Community work
Two

edited by **David Jones**
Principal, National Institute for Social Work

and

Marjorie Mayo
Lecturer in Community Work, University of Surrey

Routledge & Kegan Paul
London and Boston

First published in 1975
by Routledge & Kegan Paul Ltd
Broadway House, 68—74 Carter Lane,
London EC4V 5EL and
9 Park Street,
Boston, Mass. 02108, USA

Set in Journal by Autoset and printed in
Great Britain by Unwin Brothers Limited

ISBN 0 7100 8191 X (c)
ISBN 0 7100 8192 8 (p)

Contents

Contributors

David Jones is Principal of the National Institute for Social Work.

Marjorie Mayo is a lecturer on the Applied Social Studies Course at the University of Surrey.

Paul Curno is on the staff of the Central Council for Education and Training in Social Work, and is a member of the Editorial Board for this series.

S. M. Miller is Chairperson of the Department of Sociology, Boston University.

Martin Rein is Professor of Social Policy, Department of Urban Studies and Planning, Massachusetts Institute of Technology.

Hilary Rose and Jalna Hanmer are both lecturers in the Department of Social Administration, London School of Economics.

Laurence Tasker is lecturer in the Department of Social Administration, University College, Swansea.

Sidney Jacobs is a research officer at the Race Relations Board. He was formerly a community worker working with tenants' groups in Glasgow.

Nicholas Derricourt and D. J. Cox are lecturers in the Department of Economics and Social Science, City of Birmingham Polytechnic.

George Goetschius, author of *Working with Community Groups*, was formerly a lecturer at the London School of Economics.

John Ward is Head of the Training Department at the National Council of Social Service.

Janet Evanson and Iain Watkinson work in 'Grapevine'—a Family Planning Association project.

David Thomas teaches community work at the National Institute for Social Work.

Graham Richies was until recently Warden of Liverpool University Settlement.

Ray Lees is the Director of the Research Team for the Batley Community Development Project.

John Greve is Professor of Social Administration at Leeds University, and was formerly Central Director of Research for the Community Development Project.

Liz Durkin, a former social worker and lecturer in social work, was involved in the Paddington Day Hospital protest group and in the formation of the Mental Patients' Union, which was launched in 1973 to fight for mental patients' rights.

Brian Douieb, a production worker at Vauxhalls. He is a member of the pilot committee for a mental patients' union and an ex-member of the M P U co-ordinating committee.

Betty Harrison is a former trade union official. Since retirement, she has been active in the old age pensioners' movement.

Introduction

David Jones, Marjorie Mayo and Paul Curno

In the Introduction to volume One we referred to the rapid expansion in community work and began to look at some of the implications of this, but in retrospect it has become clear that we need to take this discussion much further. Events of the past year or so have even more clearly emphasised this need to examine the significance and direction of current developments, the pressures behind them, the challenges before them.

Increasingly community work has become the object of government interest, not just for any intrinsic merit but more particularly because of its supposed contribution to the resolution of the problems of 'urban deprivation' in the 'inner city'. The creation of the Urban Deprivation Unit in the Home Office and the announcement of the comprehensive community projects are part of this trend. Without going into the reasons for this development in detail here, it would nevertheless seem important at least to summarise them.

Governments have been under pressure because of the seriousness of these problems, which can no longer be conceptualised solely as reflecting the personal inadequacies of the people involved or as dwindling pockets within the context of overall affluence, but which have increasingly had to be recognised as the symptoms of more fundamental problems of continued material and political inequality in western societies. There has also been more pressure because of the greater public awareness of the problems, and higher popular aspirations. So, governments have needed to look for new solutions although because of scarce resources, exacerbated by world-wide inflation, they have also been forced to look for solutions on the cheap. At the same time, governments have been seeking to reform administrative and political systems for a variety of reasons, including a need to revive popular confidence in these institutions, to give them credibility—hence the interest in 'participation' programmes, for instance.

To all these pressures, 'community development' has appeared as a *deus ex machina*—a tailor-made solution—self-help being relatively cheap, at least compared with some other solutions to urban deprivation, as well as being politically ambiguous and attractively populist, which appeals to the liberal, predominantly middle-class, professional lobby.

Volume One already dealt with some of these aspects of community programmes—for instance Adah Kay's chapter, 'Planning, Participation and Planners' located participation programmes in the sphere of political struggle, and John Benington explained the reasons for the Coventry Community Development Project team's rejection of the original CDP dialogue approach involving the problems of tokenism and co-optation.

These negative and double-edged aspects of official sponsorship of community development are further discussed in the first section of this year's volume—both in theoretical terms in the chapters by Miller and Rein, and Rose and Hanmer, for instance and, more practically, by Sid Jacobs. Some of the intractable problems in relation to the evaluation of such programmes are also discussed in the section on research.

These developments have within them their own contradictions— first, by the very fact that governments genuinely need these programmes, they also need to support various aspects of them, even including some which they would perhaps prefer not to. Thus even the most narrowly conceived programmes may result in some real improvements. In addition, they contain contradictions because, for a variety of reasons, the programmes have appealed to a variety of radicals and reformers in a number of professions and occupations (partly mirrored in the chapters in *Community Work One* and, in this volume, on community development in other professions and institutions including health education, for example). They also have involved indigenous residents, and this has been a new factor contributing to the pressure for change. For alongside the official growth of interest in community development programmes, and out of the same soil, have come developing grass-roots movements.

The increasingly severe housing crisis in some areas, the inadequacies of social security payments and pensions in the face of rising inflation, the shortcomings of the schools, and recreation facilities for children and young people in deprived inner-city localities—these and all the other instances of the increasingly felt inadequacies of the welfare state have been producing their own reactions in the form of growing popular protest organisations such as tenants' associations, parent-teacher associations, pensioners' and claimants' unions and a host of other consumer groups.

Students, young professionals and the 'alternative culture' have also been important ingredients, for example, in the rise of claimants' unions. But popular protest movements have also included a core of working-class tenants, pensioners and parents who are forced to organise to defend their own immediate interests. In this sense, for them, community development is not an extracurricular activity or even an alternative to other more effective forms of political activity at the workplace, but the only option open to them.

Given these ambiguous expectations for change through community projects, it remains obvious enough that the present enthusiasm for community development cannot be expected to last. The projects cannot, on their own, possibly solve the material problems of the inner city, let alone the wider problems of economic and political inequality. As several of the chapters make clear (e.g. Tasker, Goetschius, Harrison), fundamental economic and political issues can ultimately be tackled only by political action on a national and indeed international level. Yet by their very nature, such projects—instead of producing any neutral, apolitical solutions—may stimulate popular protest organisations. So when this basic reality is officially recognised in relation to community development, and the early unrealistic expectations are publicly shattered, some kind of reaction is only to be expected. In addition, the level of demands on the welfare state and the pressures for stringency in public spending, which arise from the present economic situation, are unlikely to disappear. The consequences for social services departments, with their increasing number of clients and caseloads for the not-so-rapidly increasing social work staff and facilities, would seem to be reinforcing the potential value of the community development approach. If you cannot provide casework services for individuals and families on your burgeoning caseload, you might as well invite them into a local self-help group, at the very least, and have hope in 'the community'. Despite the Association of Community Workers' guidelines for the appointment of community workers (Notes for Employers, prepared by the ACW in November 1973), the work situation of new recruits is frequently fraught with ambiguities and contradictions of this nature. Community work, in terms both of participation and of planning, is an essential component of the enlarged Seebohm conception of the role and responsibilities of the personal social services. Similar considerations are increasingly emphasised in many other fields of activity.

It may also be worth while for the community worker to point out to governments and local authorities some of the reasons why they will still need community development programmes, even after they have discovered their limitations. The clock may be turned back, in the short term; but, in the long term, if the last thirty or forty years are anything to judge from, the scale of public intervention, both in the economy in general and in social welfare in particular, cannot easily be reversed. Especially with the growth of larger 'rationalised' units of administration—as with local government and health service reorganisation—the need for popular and locally based participation programmes can also be expected to increase. For whether these do or do not offer any challenge to existing arrangements, they may still be considered increasingly necessary on the level of communication, rational and efficient administration and/or co-optation of popular protest, however uncomfortable for the authorities concerned.

In face of this situation several authors, both in this volume (e.g. Goetschius, Tasker) and in last year's (e.g. Bryant) make references to the importance of community workers' growing political awareness. Clearly, they must indeed develop this if they are to be at all effective in working with local groups which have to operate, whether consciously or not, within a *political* context, in the broadest sense of the term (i.e. concerned with power and the distribution of resources).

But this is very different from advocating (as some authors have done) that community workers should themselves become political educators or leaders in their professional capacity as community workers. Skill and knowledge they must have—but by what mandate should they, or could they, exercise that very different characteristic, political leadership? Clients' rejection of leadership by the community worker is abundantly clearly emphasised in chapter 12 in the section contributed by the grass-roots organisations themselves.

Meanwhile, in the short term, many community workers may come to feel inadequate, isolated and under attack. This relates to a further theme embarked on in this volume—the desirable future development and training of the community work profession itself.

On the one hand, some community workers feel that 'professionalism', and hence training, must be rejected on the grounds that they represent merely restrictive practices to benefit the collective self-interest of a newly emerging elite—and that, as such, professionalism is anti 'the people'. It is seen as a claim to exclusive knowledge and expertise and a denial of the value community work places on self-determination, the sharing of knowledge and skill and helping people to help themselves rather than remaining dependent on professional intervention. On the other hand, 'going to the people' without an appropriate organisational mandate, in terms both of the organisation's purposes and of the worker's role within the organisation, is likely to land the individual practitioner in difficulties. At this point, workers may attempt to legitimise their activities by an appeal to principles and skill and begin to seek support from professional colleagues, or even in the mere possession of professional credentials. But beyond this, many community workers are deeply concerned to increase their knowledge and skill in order to serve more effectively those they are working with. Hence the ambivalence towards professionalism among many workers, which at its extreme leads to a rejection of training, coupled with a desire for a qualification. Analagous contradictions are inherent in the development of courses for non-professional indigenous community workers, a subject we hope to examine in the next volume.

The implication of the Cox and Derricourt chapter would seem to be that, whether trained or untrained, or organised as an avowedly professional body or not, community workers are unlikely ever to acquire bargaining power on a par with the older professions such as medicine and law. If such is the reality of the situation, from where should community workers obtain support? Do they have to rely solely on their own knowledge, skill and personal integrity or the support of their employing organisation, or should they look also to recognised training and professional organisations?

Many professionals in human service occupations, particularly those in bureaucratic organisations, are members both of a professional body and a trade union or participate in some hybrid arrangement. Many community workers will, in fact, have prior or concurrent membership of other professional bodies and trade unions. Given the development of community work in many different professional and organisational settings, this may be necessary and desirable. Trade union membership is likely to be the most appropriate way of promoting the collective self-interest of community workers in terms of rewards and conditions of service. Professional bodies, too, may be much involved with the collective interests of their members—excessively so, according to their critics—but they are also much more likely to be concerned with issues of role definition and standards of competence. As far as community workers are concerned, the issue of professional organisation is further complicated by the fact that although community work may be a logical and inherent development of many different professional activities, for most professional organisations it is yet merely of peripheral interest. These are major issues to be taken into account by the ACW as it considers its future development.

The editors would argue that empathy with 'the people', even empathy with 'deprived people' or 'the working class', is no substitute for a realistic strategy for contemporary community work in face of the increasingly complex dilemmas of state intervention in welfare and community in advanced industrial societies, particularly at a time of nil or negative growth.

Part I Community Work Participation and Politics

1 Community participation: past and future

S.M. Miller and Martin Rein

The emergence of participation

Why did participation emerge in the United States during the late 1960s as a big-city, black, and disadvantaged issue? Although it is difficult in the seventies to recapture the sources of discontent in the urban scene, at the beginning of the sixties one precipitating event can be identified. The black and minority population of big cities was rapidly increasing, both absolutely and relatively, in the big cities. Lacking effective organization, they were ignored by the established political power centers and abused by efforts to renew cities where it had the effect of removing Negroes from downtown districts and areas surrounding urban universities. While the growing size and poor treatment of new urban residents is basic to the development of the participation story, the more immediate causal agents were the civil rights movement in the South and the decisions of the Supreme Court (school desegregation, one man one vote, etc.) which gave the movement legal support and nourishment.

Two processes of decay contributed to this poor treatment—the weakness of the political machine and the ineffectiveness of municipal agencies. Each reinforced the other.

> Destruction of the party foundation of the mayorality cleaned up many cities but also destroyed the basis of sustained, central, popularly-based action. This capacity with all its faults was replaced by the power of professionalized agencies . . . The modern city has become well-run but ungoverned because it has . . . become comprised of 'islands of functional power' before which the modern mayor stands denuded of authority.[1]

Earlier, the political machine of the big cities had brought ethnic

3

minorities into the electoral mainstream. The long erosion of power
of the machine meant that it was less adaptive to new groups and less
able to provide patronage for allegiance. Black citizens were by and
large not represented in the councils of power, or were represented
by persons without loyalty to improve racial conditions. Black
appointees in machines lacked even a dual allegiance to build racial
as well as personal power. Where the machine was strongest, as in
Chicago, community participation was fought by the Democratic
Party mayor. In New York City, by contrast, a Republican Party
mayor began to build new sources of local support in board
participation and encouraged its development. But some machines
at the neighborhood level fought Mobilization for Youth in the
Lower East Side of New York because of its efforts to organize a
voter registration campaign which might have threatened the power
of the older ethnic group which controlled the local machine and its
patronage. Machine politics and community participation are thus
closely meshed. Established political power fought it in some cities,
controlled it in others, and encouraged its autonomy where political
expediency required it. But participation emerged from the efforts
to defend political democracy. Although it was responded to in
many different ways, the drive for participation was an effort to
expand and defend the concept of democracy so that low-income
citizens had more opportunity to affect the political decisions which
affected them.

The second process which fed the development of community
participation was the malperformance in the administrative agencies
which serviced the poor and the ghettos in the fifties and early
sixties. Municipal services such as sanitation and police were
deteriorating; schools failed to open opportunity and, by responding
to white expectations, reaffirmed black incapacity, while manpower
programs and job referrals never reached the poor from the outset.
Social service agencies had disengaged from the poor. The
employment problems of black ghettos were not being met.
Administrative decisions had more far-reaching consequences than
city council decisions and were less accountable to redress by
aggrieved citizens. The big-city financial crisis aggravated the
administrative crises.

The symptoms of neglect were interpreted largely in terms of
self-regarding professionals in the human services. The academic
credentials which certified professional competence seemed to
reaffirm black incompetence. Rainwater called these professionals

'the dirty workers' of society, because they blundered in social action and inspired a crisis of personal identity and self-confidence. There was an irony in the insistence on professional credentials, for it wounded the esteem and dignity of the poor. Credentialism, professionalism and the bureaucracies which spawned them became widely regarded as the villains causing the decay of low-income communities. Participation was to be an important element in the demand for institutional change and for curbing irresponsible professionals who 'cashed in'. This is gained from the efforts to aid the poor communities without providing them with help in return for their winnings.

To cope with the deficiencies of representation and responsiveness, new resources appeared. Meager at first in the comprehensive planning projects of the President's Committee on Juvenile Delinquency and the Gray Area projects of the Ford Foundation,[2] they grew more impressive in the mid-sixties in the Economic Opportunity Act, Model Cities legislation, Community Mental Health Act and other programs. Since these new programs had limited prior planning nationally and almost none locally, a major issue was how to convert the possibilities of money into the realities of programs. But the external war in Vietnam soon nullified the growth of the internal war against urban poverty. Before this grim prognosis was understood, planning became the important local activity. Who was to plan and who was to run programs became key issues. The outpouring of planning funds and the possibilities of much greater operating resources raised the sums in big cities and made the fight for participation and control much more significant than when shifts were made within an insufficient and slowly expanding fiscal pie.

The struggle for planning took place in and contributed to the context of a profound change in the social and political climate of black and other minority communities. A new minority consciousness, pride and identity emerged. Black Power was the most dramatic manifestation of it. When local planning, encouraged by federal resources, merged with Black Power, it led to the demand for self-determination, defined as control of the decision-making and administrative apparatus.

In summary, the demand for participation sprang from the failures of democracy and bureaucracy, but it was encouraged as well by the new possibilities and new expectations which the failures had inspired. The failures were in the traditional political machinery

and administrative structures; the new possibilities were those of
federal resources to the cities. The new expectations found
expression in three specific goals and in the diversity of activities
developed to realize these aims.

The support for participation

The support for participation can be categorized in terms of three
contrasting aims—changing people, changing institutions and
changing groups.

Changing people

The community action programs of the Office of Economic
Opportunity gave rise to the difficult and disturbing formula of
'maximum feasible participation' of the residents of poverty areas in
the development and operation of programs aimed to eliminate their
poverty. Many of those involved in the development of the
Economic Opportunity Act regarded participation as therapeutic,
overcoming the spiritual emptiness of ghetto life and the apathy of
the poor. Alienated from the norms of society, the poor were seen
as retreating into a protective subculture of poverty characterized by
social disengagement and indifference. Kenneth B. Clark, a leading
black psychologist and figure, has described the stagnation of the
poor as their most striking characteristic. The poor have a pervasive
sense of futility, which, according to Clark, is not even positive
enough to be called cynical. It follows that it is hard to disillusion the
poor, for they start with few illusions. Equally, it is hard to engage
the poor, for they start with few hopes. It is this theme which
explains why Harlem Youth Opportunities Unlimited (H A R Y O U),[3]
led by Clark—the predecessor of the community action agency in
Harlem—assigned crucial importance to the idea of culture-building.
The destruction of culture can be understood, as the subtitle of their
planning report suggests, as 'the consequence of powerlessness'. The
lack of power derives from the black's dependence, the inability to
control the events which shape his life without the aid of whites.

The consequence and self-respect of the black was to be achieved
by his own involvement and participation in shaping and creating his
own life; it was the young who would provide the source of
leadership. Poverty is caused by powerlessness, and the means to
overcome poverty is self-help and participation. The more the black

himself operated the strategic institutions in ghetto life, the more he would be able to reject welfare colonialism and substitute a vital independence and self-respect, the more would poverty, defined as powerlessness, decline.

This point of view stresses that poverty is not so much a lack of material advantage, in the sense of insufficient economic resources, as it is a lack of power. It assumes that there was something wrong with the poor which left them unprepared to exploit the resources and opportunities available to them. Hence, what was needed was a program to prepare the poor so that they could more effectively use available community institutions and resources. Remediation, employability and citizen participation programs were needed to achieve this aim. All of these programs share a common rationale—the reduction of the dependence and the apathy of the poor in order to give the poor the opportunity to participate in the mainstream of American society. While participation played a prominent role in the early statements of the Office of Economic Opportunity (OEO), the federal anti-poverty agency, the dominating hallmark of its operating programs was training—training for work habits, training for skill development, training for citizenship and training for participation.

The poverty program, then, was essentially concerned with promoting compliance with American norms. The link between power and conformity was contained in the ideal of trying to promote a competent community. Residents of a community should be able to solve their own problems and control their own destinies by being able to influence the institutions which service them. When those who reside in an area lose the capacity to solve their own problems or the capacity to modify institutional performance in accordance with their needs, a breakdown in the institution of authority frequently results. This weakness in turn erodes mechanisms of social control. The grim product of the incompetent community is the collapse of its control system. Institutional incompetence leads to personal incompetence, with the consequences of the growth of crime, delinquency and social deviancy.

Apathy among the poor prevents them from effectively demanding that the institutions which service them accommodate to their needs. The result is that their plight worsens and their capacity for effective action is further weakened. A vicious cycle of poverty reinforces a vicious cycle of bureaucratic dysfunction. To break the cycle, the vigor of local democracy must be restored, and this can best be accomplished by expanding the freedom and the competence of local residents to respond to their local problems. Citizen involvement in local decision-making, through competent local leaders who understand how best to command the events and institutions which shape the lives of the poor, is a major ingredient of the strategy of building a competent community on the assumption that people change as they try to change their world.

Black communities in the mid-sixties rejected this early sociotherapeutic view of participation. They pushed for participation as power rather than as cure. But the sociotherapeutic approach is sturdy and reappears in new dress.

Changing institutions

In almost every area of service, the level of performance in poor black areas was lower than in more affluent or in white areas. In education, less was spent per student and each dollar was utilized with less effectiveness than in the white sections of most cities. Sanitation pick-ups were usually less frequent, traffic controls less stringent.

Planning for the future of minority communities frequently tended to disregard the felt needs of the residents. Instead, city-wide rather than neighborhood interests determined their design and location. The most striking illustration is that of urban renewal, which decreased the number of low-rent dwelling units, replacing them with a smaller number of expensive units and office buildings. As a result, urban renewal was tarred as 'Negro removal'.

Black communities saw themselves as suffering from poor performance and poor planning. A third cause of attack on the planning and operating agencies was that they were largely manned by whites at both the decision-making and personnel levels.

What evolved in the sixties were ways of dealing with these issues of accountability, planning and employment. In employment, the non-professional emerged as a powerful social invention. This new occupational role not only provided employment opportunities for residents, a need inadequately met by most OEO programs, but also promised to improve the educational and social services by bridging the gap between the professional provider and skeptical neighborhood residents. And it provided one way for community residents to be involved in the service agency. But progress was uneven.

In the spring of 1969 about one-third of twenty community action agencies studied had hired no non-professional workers. While clearly no universal pattern emerged, it was equally obvious that in the remaining two-thirds of the agencies non-professionals were numerically important. One-third employed thirty or more non-professionals and one-third had employed seventy or more. These non-professionals were women (24%), blacks (67%) and residents of the target areas (86%).[4]

With the explosion of planning for change, two difficulties became painfully clear: the technical base of planning was inadequate; planning cannot supersede the question of values.

Technical support for planning was more often absent than present. What kinds of measures have what effects? Will Headstart programs for pre-school children have a greater payoff in terms of children's school performance than later compensatory education, or raising the incomes of families without changing schools? We simply do not know the answer. Or consider a less ultimate question. What are the best ways of institutionalizing programs? Is it more effective to organize social services around the ages of users (e.g. aged, children) than on the nature of the service (e.g. preventive, supportive)? No one was sure of the respective yields.

The problem is not only how to achieve specified goals, but which goals are primary. Political support for a general line of action is usually secured by ambiguity in statement of goals and the cloaking of the conflict among them. When more specific planning or action occurs, the underlying disagreements emerge. Any planning act helps some more than others; seldom do all benefit equally. Consequently, even highly competent professionals do not have scientific rules for decision-making which can substitute for the political will.

The limits of science reinforce the importance of community participation in the planning process. Participation affirms broad principles of intent and sets priorities, while science provides presumably the means for their implementation. This division of responsibility between the purposes of intervention and the strategy to realize the social values on which meaning and purpose are predicated is ancient. The dominant theory of bureaucratic accountability depends on it. What was unique about planning designed to promote change and improve the machinery of bureaucratic accountability in the sixties was that different types of citizens were allowed in or, more accurately, demanded entrance into the new planning process. These poor, black residents, once treated as clients without power, were now asserting claims and rights as citizens which redefined the traditional separation between lay and professional authority. They not only ratified, rejected or modified plans, they sometimes submitted different plans built on value premises which competed with those of the professionals or political leaders.

The push for accountability sprang from the indictment of the poor performance of agencies presumably servicing low-income and black communities. As planning moved to implementation, there was growing concern for what happens day-to-day in the community. Professionals and administrators in agencies could not be depended upon to keep the interests of the low-income community foremost in their actions. Personal, bureaucratic, professional and city-wide concerns duel for supremacy with the commitment to the deprived community. The need, then, was for mechanisms to produce accountability to the community of service users.

The move toward authentic involvement in planning and operations required that at least some disadvantaged citizens command positions of authority. Poor, black citizens began to sit on the central planning committees, on local advisory boards and on the staff of planning and service agencies. This theory of accountability repudiates the principle of professional objectivity and elite disinterest. Leading citizens sit on boards as presumably representing 'the public interest' in which they have no monetary or financial stake. It is based upon a vague notion of declared interest of the consumer. Poor or black residents first sought accountability by publicly criticizing agencies for malperformance (as defined by the residents). Aggressive measures, such as demonstrations and sit-ins were used.* With the growth of resources and political pressure, residents moved into positions on boards (a decentralized school board) and agencies (community action agency) where they had an

---

* These actions created great turmoil among the political machine partisans who viewed them as a breach of faith or at least a violation of the rules of the political game. Letting blacks into positions formerly denied them should have meant that they accepted the conventions of electoral and machine politics. Disputes were resolved within the machine and by machine people. 'Going to the streets', confrontations and sit-ins—what Piven has called 'dissensus' or 'confrontational politics', as opposed to electoral politics, was considered bad form, a violation of the rules. Black communities, however, viewed confrontational politics as their means to dramatize, intimidate and mobilize support for their case. Confrontational politics also became the road to leadership to those in the black communities aspiring for power roles within these communities. See the discussion below of participation and service delivery.

institutionalized, legitimized base for questioning the performance of the agency. A fulcrum for changing institutions emerged or, as some critics maintain, a fulcrum for maintaining equilibrium by cooling off passions by promising pseudo-authority.

Both a pseudo-transfer of power and a transfer of pseudo-power frequently occurred. But participation did lead to some changes in the source of power as well as in service delivery and performance. Marcia Guttentag[5] argues that community control, which has been widely and sometimes eagerly judged as a failure, was a success. The findings of later research are different from those of early studies. One of the aims (and many have argued, the prime aim) was to change the behavior, aspirations and attitudes of ghetto residents through a strategy of participation. People change as they try to change their world. While the Harlem experiment with community-controlled schools created deep conflict between professionals and consumers, it also changed the aspirations of adults and increased the educational achievement of the children who participated in it.

PARTICIPATION OR ACOUNTABILITY

Changing groups

'Participation' in the sixties was largely a big-city issue and, within the big cities, an issue for blacks and other disadvantaged minorities. (To a large extent, the term 'disadvantaged' served as a substitute for black.) While some of the initial support for it came from those concerned, as we have said, with sociotherapy, the residents of 'disadvantaged' areas did not share this interest. Their outlook was that of power. Some sought to gain in political power while they improved economically; indeed, many believed that the long-term prospect of economic gain depended on the growth of political power. The 'Black Revolution' was central to the participation issue.

The power issue emerged in two principal ways: as equity and as self-determination. The equity view holds that the disadvantaged in city centers should have the same advantages as the suburban advantaged, and that income is not a ground for discriminatory treatment. In suburbs, citizens are on the school boards which make decisions; they are elected to the august board of selectmen which makes basic-level decisions. Because of the size of large cities and the legacy of political exclusion, the disadvantaged (who are concentrated in the big cities) do not have these possibilities. New structures (e.g. school decentralization) are needed to make participation possible for the disadvantaged. 'American democracy' is more than a symbol in the suburbs; in the city, it is a mockery to the disadvantaged.

We are not sure that democracy is as widespread in the suburbs as the equity argument implies, but certainly it is more evident than in the metropolis. To some extent, the effort at participation in the cities forges new kinds of institutions which permit different links between citizen and government. These new institutional forms will probably be of value in both suburbs and city although more important in the city, where disadvantaged citizens especially are cut off from the making of decisions.

The self-determination argument goes beyond the equity position. Separatist black institutions were called for, sometimes as an interim step to build up black identity and power, sometimes as a permanent form to give blacks control over their 'turf' with no connection with the rest of the city.

Today, the principle of territoriality leads to separatism because blacks and other minority groups are geographically concentrated and segregated. But the *purpose* of greater control over one's area may not be to promote separatism but to promote equity and to win greater resources.

Criticisms of participation

By outlining the movement towards participation and its evolution, we have tried to make a case that it contributes importantly and positively to the various goals reviewed. But strong criticisms of the drive for participation have emerged. We discuss these doubts around four points: participation and service delivery, planning and accountability, democracy, and authenticity.

Participation and service delivery

Most experience with participation in the sixties was at the planning stage. Where there was participation at the operational stage, as in CAP programs, the delivery of services was characterized frequently as ineffective.

Although community participation and the more effective delivery of services are linked in the minds of many, they are frequently in conflict. The participation strategy, designed to promote quality, may in fact erode the quality of available services.

It is important to recognize that improving public services is not easy. The long-term general situation of many low-income communities and neighborhoods is that they have long suffered from inadequate services. (Some would argue, using the post office as an example, that poor delivery is not restricted to poor neighborhoods.) In any case, new organizations and leaders usually encounter difficulties in performing. Discussion may be delayed because of the excessive concern with having all issues, even very minor or detailed ones, debated and acted upon by the representatives of the residents. Conflicts may flourish, with the consequent making and unmaking of decisions. Inappropriate decisions may be made. Incompetent administrators may be chosen on political grounds. More important perhaps is that even highly committed personnel may be unable to overcome the basic lack of resources to meet local needs.

Hopefully, with some experience, delivery will improve. The decentralized model common to many forms of participation may eventually permit (a) more effective coordination at the neighborhood level of now disjointed services and (b) the development of more relevant services.

The second type of criticism against linking participation from the main political contribution is that participation can contribute to ghetto improvement. Piven has been an eloquent spokesman for this position. If the unequal share of resources is the major problem of the ghetto, then confrontation and dissensus politics will increase the cost to the white community of maintaining this inequality and underfunding. While the resources may be poorly used (inefficiency) or may not altogether be relevant (ineffectiveness), still the adequacy of resources is an essential precondition for their use. Adequacy facilitates efficiency and may also overcome ineffectiveness. If inadequate resources cause fundamental and insurmountable problems, then service participation is not only distracting, but undermining as well. By directing energies to the use of present resources, participation may hinder the task of acquiring substantial new resources.

The choice seems to be between two different conceptions of participation. Political participation argues for the creation of effective political organization to make demands, while allocative operational participation is preoccupied with the distribution and use of resources already in hand. The history of participation in the poverty program shows that each without the other is insufficient, but both cannot be combined without great strain.

The difficulties in creating political organization in San Francisco propelled the program into a service strategy as a way of attracting supporters. While Mobilization for Youth (MFY) in New York City moved in the other direction, it began essentially to make a service strategy and was driven to reassess its role in community participation. The community organization program accounted for less than 5 per cent of the resources spent by MFY. But the resistances of established agencies and the insufficiency of resources drove MFY to allocate more of its resources to the organization neighborhood groups. The resulting conflict between the political and service strategies was sharp and clear. Some argued that a choice must be made, and opted for organization and subordination of services. For a short while the political strategy prevailed, but the organization soon surrendered the gain to a service approach.

Each strategy of participation without the other is insufficient, yet they collide when pursued within the same organizational structure. The Welfare Rights Movement, committed to the creation of political organization among welfare recipients as a strategy of winning more resources and a more humane and adequate welfare system, confronted this dilemma. The national office accepted a quarter of a million dollars manpower grant in the Work Incentive Program, a job training program for women receiving welfare payments. The Pennsylvania chapter revolted, arguing that commitment to the running of a service program would undermine the organizing and confrontational tasks of the movement.

Each organization committed to participation faces at some point in its history the need to make a choice between operating to deliver service or engaging in political combat to win resources and change. Public policy at the national level must decide whether it wishes to mix or keep separate these competing and complementary conceptions of participation.

To the extent that service agencies cannot effectively function in minority, low-income areas without a high degree of participation, moves toward participation will emerge, even if at the sacrifice of some performance.

Planning and accountability

Local participation presents two issues of accountability: the conflict between staff and board. The theory of the accountability of public bureaucracies touches simultaneously on the theories of bureaucracy and of democracy. Accountability calls for a procedure for the review of both the internal decisions of a bureaucracy and of the consequences of bureaucratic action on the broader objectives of public policy (e.g. social or educational utilization; equality in expenditures among neighborhoods; or equal employment opportunities). In principle, the mayor appoints the board of a public agency and they are accountable to him; the staff of the agency in turn carry out the policy of the board and are responsible to them. Aggrieved clients or the disillusioned can appeal to the board and to the mayor. If they do not get satisfaction, they can elect a new mayor. The policy of the board and the mayor must take account of local needs and city-wide interests, but such an accounting in these theories does not require deep citizen involvement, only the chance of voters to present government and to review at some point the general performance of the elected officials who are held to be responsible.

But the theories have worked out poorly for the ghetto, and consequently new rationales have emerged with a new set of opportunities and difficulties concerning the role of the citizen, especially the resident of low-income areas.

Do poorly-educated citizens have the competence to participate in planning? The experience of Community Action and Model Cities programs strongly points to the conclusion that they do. But that is not to say that technical competence is not needed or that residents are exclusive repositories of the wisdom of what needs to be done and how in low-income communities. What has emerged is that ordinary citizens not only have usefully functioned to review plans developed by experts but have an important contribution to make at the level of the development of the plan. They are different kinds of 'experts' from the technically trained, college-educated genre.

In short, residents have an important but not exclusive role in planning. The model of advocate planners has developed a new relationship between residents and experts, in that experts now accept the leadership of low-income citizens, as earlier they accepted the obligation to operate within the mandates of their political, commercial or bureaucratic employers. The dominant role frequently no longer belongs to the professional or political head of an agency, but to that of the community's poorly-educated leaders. This model gives citizens a new role in planning in which they offer alternatives and competition to elite-derived plans.

One hoped-for result is that better plans will emerge from the competition of alternatives. Another contrasting result is inaction, as competing groups battle and the veto power of each group stops the activities of all. The Model City experience has been encouraging, in that most cities have been able to end up with a plan which merged neighborhood and other interests. While successful civic entrepreneurs like Robert Moses and Edward Logue regarded citizen participation as one of the main barriers to action, more citizen involvement than in the past is needed if the interests of the disadvantaged and the poor are not to be submerged in larger (usually more narrowly economic) considerations.

A second type of criticism of participation in planning is that the neighborhood is not an appropriate unit for which to plan. How can a highway system or even a hospital system be planned only in relation to the needs and preferences of a neighborhood? In the former, the operation of the whole metropolitan area must be considered; in the latter, the distribution of labor in terms of specialties (does every hospital need a heart transplant facility?) is required for efficient deployment of scarce resources.

There is obvious merit in this contention, and it will be necessary to develop at least temporary alliances and coalitions among neighborhood units. Even metropolitan government is compatible with greater neighborhood participation; the neighborhood organizations and the formal governmental units of cities and towns can link up for some joint actions. But undoubtedly this development is difficult; metropolitan government has been achieved in very few places and inter-governmental compacts are scarce indeed. Hopefully, experience will drive even inwardly-oriented neighborhood units to respond to the need for joint action on a broader scale.

A third type of criticism is the undermining of the authority, and therefore the accountability, of the traditional city government. If mayors cannot make decisions, they cannot be held accountable: a common experience in many cities where power is already highly fragmented so that no one can be charged with the responsibility for failure.

Mechanisms will have to be developed to make neighborhood organizations more accountable. Election procedures are one way, but they have not been very effective as yet with their low turnouts. In Model City programs in some cities, turnouts have been higher. As issues emerge and performance can be judged, elections can become more important.

In the community control version of participation, policy is set independently of city-wide concerns so that it can be most responsive to the demands of the ghetto. What is being called for is a separation between fiscal accountability (city, state, and federal) and administrative policy. Central bureaucracy tends stubbornly to resist the demands for autonomy. Local groups have secured resources with the support of federal agencies which offered them some basis of independence. The need for institutional change legitimates such steps. Three different approaches to neighborhood bureaucracies have been tried:

(a) *Parallelism:* a parallel activity program is developed which essentially carries out functions similar to those of the public bureaucracy, but under alternative auspices, e.g. Opportunities Industrialization Centers conducting vocational education programs run through the school system.

(b) *Outpost* of public bureaucracy: a local branch office is established with power to modify city-wide policy to the advantage of the local neighborhood (Model Cities).

(c) *Community control:* a mixture of (a) and (b). In the case of decentralized school districts in New York City, the financing has been at the city level with appropriations to the districts; the hiring of personnel is at the district level following city requirements and pay scales; the tenure of the teachers is city-wide; branch policy is a combination of city and state decisions with the growing importance of the districts.

Each approach poses special difficulties and opportunities; parallelism offers opportunity for experimentation but makes the system more complex and overlapping. Outposts can readily present an illusion of change with the reality of stability. Control reinforces racial, ethnic and class separatism, while it caters to local tastes.

Democracy
PARTICIP   UNDEMOC
The issue of democracy shades off from the question of accountability. Who is to plan, who is to represent the community, how is he or she to be checked? What is the 'community'; who is in it?

Voting is a procedure for selection of members to represent the community on the boards of community action agencies or neighborhood committees. The appointee system was judged to be too susceptible to cooptation or to the process of 'give and take', often described as 'selling out' and 'buying in'.* The decision to use elective machinery posed a host of inherent difficulties:

(a) Election by majority, but how to respect minorities? (The issue of proportional representation arose to assure that some groups got into office, instead of winner gets all.)

(b) The problem of accountability to constituencies, because elections preceded the development of constituencies and mechanisms to and through which elected officials could report to those who elected them.

(c) The functions of the elected official were vague, because the institution he was to function in was evolving.

'Getting out the vote' is of course the heart of the democratic procedure whereby citizens express their choices through candidates. But a democratic procedure in some areas meant supporting the Democratic Party. If only 20–30 per cent of the ghetto register and vote for the office of, say, mayor, then doubling these figures in the many ghettos of large cities could create new political alliances. The machinery used to encourage voter registration is not politically neutral. Community action programs in big cities and in the South were vulnerable to the danger that participation in voting might lead to a political redistribution of power. In the South and in some large urban areas like Chicago and New York, programs of community action agencies to increase voter registration threatened their continuation. The central government was vulnerable to the same criticism—community action was often regarded as a way of building the Kennedy–Johnson presidential machine by linking local and national politics.

It has been argued that smaller units are less likely to be democratic than larger units. The vaunted small unit, town meeting democracy of New England was frequently autocratic and excluded many residents who were marginal to the dominant community values. But it is not inevitable that smaller units, like neighborhoods, be less democratic than larger units like cities. Since the population of some 'neighborhoods' is that of a medium-sized city (150,000), smallness is not the issue. Rather, the concern is with the mechanisms by which representatives are chosen and checked—problems endemic to all governing organizations, regardless of size—and the possibilities of hearing and responding to dissident

---

* 'Selling out' is saying that the motives for an agreement or acquiescence are too small for the community and too large for the regulator; 'buying in' declares that the regulator recognizes the small gains but sees them as a step towards greater long-term gains for the community.

opinion. Since governments at all levels are charged with poor performance in these respects, it is unlikely that higher levels can be expected, at least at this point, of the new modes of participation. Participation on the basis of territoriality—residents in a geographic area—leads today to racially and ethnically distinct units. The fear is that the drive for separatism will realize its objectives in the formation of new organizational units whose constituency is all black or all Puerto Rican or all Mexican-American.

The counter-argument is that the opponents of neighborhood control of the new quasi-governmental units of community action are asking minorities to exchange any chance of greater immediate measures of power and autonomy for indefinite future hopes of integration and influence in the larger city units. It is nice to talk about an open and racially dispersed society, but as long as it is not achieved, minority groups should be able to exercise greater authority in their neighborhoods. This step runs the danger of permanent separatism. But it may be possible to offset this danger by keeping the boundaries of units fairly flexible.

Authenticity

The sixties can be seen as the time of political struggle to generate more public resources and to capture them for the black and the poor. Community participation in old or new established structures can be cooptative and may reduce the leverage which can be exercised to capture resources through dissensus or confrontational politics.[6] Participation can become an end in its own terms, rather than participation in power. For the participants may become trapped in the details of scrimping with meager resources, rather than battling for larger and larger resources.

At some points, of course, coming into the seats of government is an important and positive step for the disadvantaged. Providing direction over existing resources is important, but the criticism is accurate in that the urgent aim is to expand resources. Holding participation roles does not necessarily generate power. For strong roles, the representatives of the neighborhoods must be able to count either on the pressures of dissensus politics (which gets them into trouble as they will be operating against the power establishments at the same time that they are expected to be a part of them) or on conventional, electoral politics (where votes can be delivered). When both bases of power are weak, participation in the new structures is only limitedly effective. For example, Mayo Lindsay in May 1969 vetoed two of the three Model City program because of excessive neighborhood participation roles; the belief i that he did this in a mayoralty campaign where white backlash wa more important than black or Puerto Rican voting or confrontation Authentic participation then requires a political base; to som extent this can be acquired through the quasi-patronage of the nev institutions, but it probably requires wider political activity.

The future of participation

Participation in itself, by itself, is not a panacea. The terrifying lesson of th sixties—difficult to learn—is that there is no panacea which wil dissolve all the problems of minority groups, poverty and big cities Participation is important, both as means and end, but it also requires much more resources and much good sense in using these resources to make a great difference in the USA.

In the sixties new political forms emerged which blurred old distinctions between the public and private sectors. Subsidie provided private enterprise to influence them to hire ('hard core' individuals whom they would not ordinarily employ; the hoary federal post office moved into a public corporation form. The community corporation and decentralization have become impor tant.

Participation has become an important thread in many of the nev forms leading to novel connections between citizens and electec officials, the emergence of neglected citizens, less elitist relation between professionals and citizens. The overall movement has beer towards the demystification of government and the opening up o new citizen involvements. But the changes are not all gains; price have to be paid for these changes. And the struggle now is abou what prices should be paid.

The resolutions of the conflicts are difficult because th participation movement is characterized by diversity, fluidity anc uncertainty. Many different models now exist; each model i constantly changing and it is uncertain what are the effects of mode and change.

One of the important models in the United States involves th political and economic emergence of blacks and, more recently Puerto Ricans and Mexican-Americans. These groups demand much larger cut of the pie of power. How much and in what ways are very much at issue. If the traditional forms of voting and representative democracy work, they will exploit them. But if they fail, new forms will be sought. But what is unmistakable is the drive for changes in political relations so that these ethnic communities move to greater control over their political life-space.

The great, new political resource for power and patronage in disadvantaged communities is public services—the (now largely defunct) community action programs, the possible development of Model Cities and the community mental health programs, the increasing expenditure on schools. Consequently, the fight for power revolves about these activities, although there is interest in the decentralized control of the police and other agencies. In the politicization of social services, the effectiveness of these services for the direct consumer is frequently less crucial than their source of authority and power.

The tradition of ethnic politics applies to some extent. Mobile ethnic groups move up politically and economically by cornering a resource—a type of job (Irish policeman), a type of activity (Italian garbage collection contractors). Ethnic politicians rise and displace W A S P political establishments.

To advance the black and other minority populations, the politicization of the neighborhood resources (schools, Model Cities, community action) is being sought. One can view non-professional jobs as the equivalent of the job patronage of the old political machines; the contracts with black entrepreneurs to rebuild the ghettos under Model Cities plans can be seen as the way of extending political largesse to new potential supporters—hopefully without the graft and poor performance of contractors of the past.

There is much in this way of appraising the participation trend—ethnic politics in a new ball-park but with old policies. But that is obviously incomplete. The drive for separatism, to the extent that it exists, underlines the importance of realizing that blacks are not just another ethnic group, a little worse treated than other ethnic groups that have been making it.

Some of the other questions which participation poses are now clear, but it is difficult to answer them. In what sector of activity—e.g. sewage disposal, housing inspection, school operation—are participation forms most useful? How do technological constraints affect the nature of participation? What roles should/can residents play in decision-making? How can politicians, profes-

sionals and poor, black citizens work together? How can
participation and delivery move together rather than at cross-
pressures? How to avoid excessive, divisive repoliticization of issues
while overcoming mystifying depoliticization? How to protect the
interests of those minority individuals who do not want to move in
the same direction as the majority? What is a useful geographic unit?

It should be clear that the term 'community control' is
misleading. No activity is free of the constraints of guidelines and
regulations. The issue is the balance between city and federal
requirements, on the one hand, and local determination on the
other. The cry for participation is to push the balance more towards
the local side, but not to eliminate the other side. The rhetoric of a
few should not obscure the fact that some shifting of authority
rather than its total transformation is the issue.

The city cannot be seen apart from federal policy and funding.
With greater movement towards new forms of governing involving
community participation, the demands for funds for various
programs will grow. Governing without money is what is today
called 'Mickey Mousing'. It is pseudo-power. Cities are strapped for
funds; neighborhoods cannot generate resources. The federal
government will have to provide much more money if local
participation is to have impact.

The great issue of community participation is that which faces all
programs—what prices are the city, its politicians, its non-poor
citizens, its bureaucratic citizens, willing to pay? Decentralization of
schools means that teachers will be subjected to community
pressures which they had largely escaped until recent years in large
cities. What sacrifices of city-wide goals are acceptable to prevent the
disadvantaging of a particular group of citizens despite the advance
of more numerous groups? How is the future development of the
city discounted against present gains or inactions which protect
enclaves and worsen the prospects of future citizens?

One cannot say that all prices should be paid for the advance in
power of the presently disadvantaged. But some prices have to be
paid if there is to be a gain for those who have long been excluded.

Participation is both a goal and a means. All over the world groups
seek 'power' or 'participation' as an end in itself, concerned with
controlling their destinies and protecting themselves against
arbitrary or unresponsive rule. Student groups as well as poor groups
express their concern for greater autonomy and self-determination.
As Nathan Glazer has said, the strivings for participation and sharing

of power are world-wide: 'Clearly, they reflect some worldwide movement of dissatisfaction with the modern state and its operation.'[7] As means, participation is a way of improving decisions and operations by bringing in the consumer voice and perspective as balance to the political and professional perspectives. In the United States, participation is an issue most acutely for students and blacks. But it is a concern for all citizens who see established power as unresponsive, arbitrary or unconcerned with their ideas. We do not as yet have a sure formula for meeting effectively the participation drive, but it is clear that American society must accommodate to this concern more effectively than it has in the past. The forms of community participation that have evolved are, we think, important steps. But the particular structure is less important at this point than national and local commitment to invigorate governmental action with the involvement of citizens. The issues of power are first raised in terms of the *taming* or curbing of arbitrary power. Next, they appear as a concern with the *transfer* of power to isolated and excluded groups. Finally, they are manifested in the effort to *transform* the relations between the power-wielders and the power-recipients. All three concerns must be dealt with. Despite the clamor and terror of the sixties, some important steps were taken. But now a halting has occurred. We believe that the destruction of much community action under the Nixon administration was a temporary cessation, not a permanent closing down of the drive for neighborhood participation. The concerns are strong, even if latent, and they will re-emerge as a political issue, for they are part of the effort to redirect and recontrol the great shift of governmental power that has taken place in the last few decades.

References

1   Theodore J. Lowi, 'Machine politics—old and new', *The Public Interest*, no. 9 (Fall, 1967), pp. 83–92.
2   See Peter Marris and Martin Rein, *Dilemmas of Social Reform*, 2nd ed., London, Routledge & Kegan Paul, 1972, pp. 23–4.
3   Harlem Youth Opportunities Unlimited, 'Youth in the Ghetto' (report for President's Committee on Delinquency and Youth Crime), 1964.
4   *Community Representation in Community Action Programs*, Report no. 5, Celia Heller School, Brandeis University, March 1969, Appendix D.
5   Marcia Guttentag, 'Children in Harlem's community-controlled schools', *Journal of Social Issues*, 28 (4), 1972, p. 18.

6 R. A. Cloward and F. F. Piven, discussion of 'Dissensus Politics' and community action programs in *Regulating the Poor*, London, Tavistock, 1972.
7 *New York Times Magazine*, 27 April 1969.

2 Community participation and social change

Hilary Rose and Jalna Hanmer

This paper arises from ongoing research into community action. As participant observers, members of the team have over the past three years worked with and observed a variety of community groups from tenants' associations to squatters and claimants' unions. Often all that the groups seemed to have in common was that they were self-organised, or at least were not organised by a paid community worker: organisationally and ideologically, community groups were, and are, sharply different. While it is important to record and analyse the histories of these separate community groups, whether it is the nation-wide movement of the claimants' unions, the activity of squatting, mainly around London, or the battle against redevelopment of a small complex of streets in Sunderland, it is also important to consider their cumulative effect.[1] Essentially, these community groups are part of a burgeoning over this last decade of micro-politics, particularly within the inner city, and they require analysing as a totality of actions taking place within a given political system or sub-system.

One of the characteristics of this activity based on the neighbourhood is the belief that theory is either irrelevant or should be derived solely from practice. This belief fails to recognise that all social actors carry around in their heads theories and world views which guide, no matter how consistently or inconsistently, their actions. Consequently, analysing existing conceptions becomes at once a clearing away of false claims to scientificity and at the same time creates the possibility of developing a coherent theory of social change based in part or in whole upon the community.

This paper is therefore negative in that it criticises the type of social and political theory which has dominated the analysis of community and participation. We characterise this as a particular form of 'scientific' approach to the social sciences, and therefore begin by looking at the sociological conceptions of community and

25

the distinctive contribution of 'scientific sociology'. We then consider the views of political science on participation, and conclude with an analysis of cybernetic concepts applied to guiding social change. As exponents of this idea, we discuss the work of Etzioni as a leading theoretical sociologist, together with that of Donnison as influential in social policy analysis in Britain.

Community

We start with the concept of community and its history in the hands of academic sociology. A historical treatment tells us both about the social context which gave rise to the concept of community and also about the way in which modern scientific sociology operationalises it, and what has happened to the idea in the course of that process.[2]

For the most part, the founding fathers of sociology were conservatives who viewed certain aspects of burgeoning capitalism with distaste. In the breakdown of the old order of traditional society, they perceived the breakdown of community and, in the birth of the new, they perceived alienation. In the social relationship of community there was warmth, depth and wholeness, a profound cohesion which, while locally based, extended far beyond. Symbolised by family and village, the concept spoke with anguish of the social bonds threatened by urbanisation and industrialisation. Instead, the new order was expressed by alienation, the divorce of human beings from the things which they made, and even from themselves. Alienation was the price of the rapid intensification of the division of labour and the accumulation of capital.

It is not difficult to accept the argument that the concepts forged during the classical period had at least as close an affinity to art as to science.[3] Thus even Comte, the most heavily scientific in terms of his proclaimed methodology, sought to regenerate community in industrialising society with an amazing amalgam of neo-medieval ritual and hierarchy. These were to be introduced as sociology's essentially positive contribution towards creating a stable and scientifically based social order.[4] This positivistic strand laid down amongst these central sociological concepts by its founder was gradually to grow stronger, becoming eventually the dominant mood of sociology.

Thus, the task of understanding society was seen to require a greater range of intellectual tools than mere hypothetico-deductionism, including a moral concern with the quality of social life. Nisbet writes, 'can anyone believe that Tonnies' typology of *Gemeinschaft* and *Gesellschaft*, Weber's vision of rationalisation, Simmel's image of metropolis and Durkheim's perspective come from logico-empirical analysis as this is understood today?'[5] Equally, despite the Marxist claim that the dialectical method forms the basis for a scientific analysis of society, Marx's writings are filled with a compassionate understanding of the human significance of the break-up of the old communal order. Both his account of the painful dislocation of village life in India and of the comforts—however false—of religion, exemplify this.[6] The difference lies in that the community the conservatives sought to reintroduce looked backwards for inspiration, whereas Marx saw community not as local but transcending even national boundaries, as flowing from the class solidarity to be achieved through revolutionary practice.

Yet despite Nisbet's thesis that community retains its relevance as a key concept, as the situation where human beings have some sense of wholeness in their relationships, community as the starting-point for enquiry no longer occupies a central position in academic sociology.[7] It does, however, remain pre-eminent in various radical social theorists' writings, particularly in the libertarian tradition, but this is part of 'unofficial' sociology,[8] to which we will return.

In a recent comprehensive survey of relevant official sociology, the authors cannot bring themselves to speak of a sociology of community, as is normal for the sociology of family, education, class or religion; instead they deliberately title their book modestly *Community Studies*.[9] Under the microscope of scientific sociology, the concept retreats into confusion, to be relentlessly classified by the new Linnaeans.[10] Hillery, for example in his exhaustive review of the literature, isolated no less than ninety-four definitions of community, culminating in his conclusion that the only common feature was that 'all of the definitions deal with people'.[11] Others, such as Margaret Stacey, have argued that the topic is essentially a myth, a non-concept.[12] She claims that the confusion about community reflects the disagreement as to whether community relates to locality, a sense of belonging, or non-work relations. Instead, she suggests that an examination of a local social system, which undergoes change as a result of external factors, is potentially very much more fruitful. The suspicion that this amounts to a definition uncommonly similar to that of a typical study of a 'community' grows into conviction, when her own study of Banbury is examined, and seen to fall well within the mainstream of community studies.[13]

However, the expectation that geography or locality will determine or indicate the nature of social relations has been sharply attacked. The point has been widely made that in industrial society local and national affiliations act as the weft and warp of the social fabric, and that to suggest that community is synonymous with village is misleading.[14] Ruth Glass has acidly commented on this backward-looking posture of sociology, which detects a rural idyll within a society in which 80 per cent of the population live within a built-up urban environment.[15] Ray Pahl and Herb Gans have equally criticised the conception of a rural-urban continuum as telling us anything about *Gemeinschaft* and *Gesellschaft* relations.[16]

Indeed, most reviews of the literature conclude by suggesting that the important concept for analysing social relationships in the non-work situation is that of *network*.[17] While the work of Barnes, Clyde Mitchell and Bott is indisputably interesting and reflects the gains which may be made by the transfer of concepts from one discipline to another by analogy, the direction of the transfer is not without significance.[18] Thus the history of the concept of community begins with nineteenth-century sociology claiming it as both central and supremely social; in the hands of twentieth-century sociology, it retreats into studies of locality, becomes merely 'dealing with people', experiences a crisis as to the legitimacy of its existence and is finally replaced by a concept derived from mathematics, the most abstract and formal of all the sciences.

An important diversion to the argument

Common to all nineteenth- and twentieth-century studies of community, whether of locality or network, is the centrality of women, a point which has been virtually overlooked.[19] In an almost thrown-away sentence, Ronald Frankenberg describes one type of community study as being the industrial sociology of the housewife. In this suggestion lies the possibility of examining the social relationships associated with the activity of housework and child-rearing, and their interconnection with the situation of the man and his work, in the context of both the predominantly middle-class women's movement and also working-class community action. Certainly it is empirically readily observable that the most militant strata in both claimants' unions and squatting are women with dependent children unsupported by men. What is known as the sociology of women is virtually underdeveloped, and in many ways the most interesting work emanates from the unofficial sociology of the movement.[20] As we hope to make clear in subsequent work, to study community is to study women.

Science and sociology

While nineteenth-century sociologists were 'caught up in the major ideologies of liberalism, radicalism, and conservatism' (see Table 1), since the 1920s and 1930s, academic sociologists have fought for a conception of the discipline as neutral, value-free and scientific.[21] What has become much more apparent recently is the way in which 'scientific' sociology itself has ideological connotations. Robert Lynd in *Sociology for What?* and C. W. Mills with *The Sociological Imagination* were to raise the question of the value of this version of scientificity, but it was not until the mid- and later 1960s that the questioning became extensive and increasingly systematic.

Table 1   *Theoretical interpretations of key sociological concepts*

Conceptions of	Traditional	Liberal	Radical
Community	unified	pluralist	divided
Social change	stability	stability through continuous change	continuous and progressive
Participation	consensus	consensus through conflict	conflict
Sociological knowledge	arts/science, humanism	scientific rationality	humanism/ dialectical science

Neither the manifestly conservative such as Talcott Parsons, stressing the normative integration of society, nor the latent conservatism of the practical policy-oriented sociologists has escaped criticism. Gouldner attacked his fellows as 'living off' sociology, rather than 'living for' sociology, a point to be echoed by Nicolaus's jibe at the ASA meeting when he charged sociologists with 'having their eyes turned downwards and their palms up', a sharp reminder that, as technicians of the Welfare State, sociologists study the poor and live well.[22] But the intellectual issues lay much deeper than this. It was not merely necessary to expose the 'manifest' and 'latent' functions of sociological research or of specific gross abuses such as *Project Camelot*, but also to re-examine the epistemological basis of contemporary sociology.[23]

Certainly the epistemological legitimacy of positivistic social science, which takes its model from natural science, is increasingly under attack. Nor is the debate entirely a reconstruction of the classical debate between causal explanation and the pursuit of laws as against understanding. In so far as the methodology of the natural sciences is undergoing reappraisal, and the central Popperian dogma of falsifiability extensively challenged, if not overthrown, then social science based on this model is in reflected difficulties.

In recent years, the theory that scientists work by seeking to falsify hypotheses has come under attack from two directions. From the perspective of the history of science, Thomas Kuhn has developed the thesis that, most of the time, scientists do not in fact attempt to falsify hypotheses; instead, under the conditions of normal science, they work within the dominant paradigm or theoretical framework.[24] It is only at periods of crisis that scientists carry out scientific revolutions, throwing out the old theoretical order and replacing it with the new.

While this work has been extremely influential in changing the orientation of the sociology of science,[25] there has also been a renewed interest in examining the relationship between the socio-economic structures and the growth of scientific ideas.[26] The increased possibility of a genuinely sociological account of the growth of the scientific knowledge is not only in itself interesting, it also raises one of the major social questions of the late twentieth century concerning the nature of science and its role in contemporary society. Where once it was possible to believe that science was an integral part of the development of a more rational society, the particular mode of rationality embodied within the scientific method is now widely questioned. Ranging from the anarcho-radicalism of Roszak[27] to the critique developed by the neo-marxist school of Frankfurt,[28] the present form of scientific rationality is seen as directly contributory to the oppressive nature of science in practice. The war in Indochina, which drew on all the apparatus of contemporary science and technology, has been the apotheosis of this practice.

In this conception of science, nature is there to be dominated and exploited and not, as in a systematic or ecological view, there to be lived with harmoniously by humanity. Indeed, in so far as human beings are part of nature, science begins by 'wanting to understand man and ends by manipulating him'.[29]

Scientific sociology in practice

It is against this background that we now consider the explicitly cybernetic theory of Etzioni[30] and its pragmatic counterpart developed by David Donnison.[31] Etzioni's *The Active Society* derives from a recognition of the significance of the cybernetic revolution and its societal implications.

Because cybernetics is a generalised theory of control processes, it is in principle applicable to the question of the maintenance of order in any environment, whether inorganic or organic, biological or social.[32] Indeed, the potentiality of the new science has been widely recognised. In 1961, after nearly a decade of philosophical discussion as to the correct relationship of cybernetics to Marxism (ranging from the view that it offered a fourth dialectrical principle to the view that cybernetics operated at a lower hierarchial plane), the Communist Party of the Soviet Union endorsed cybernetics as a major tool in the construction of a communist society. A cybernetic system seemed to offer the USSR precisely what had become unmanageably lost in the pre-cybernetic top-heavy and unresponsive bureaucracies—or, in cybernetic language, lost in the increasing entropy of the system.[33]

Cybernetics, fundamentally, is a system of information collection, storage and analysis. When applied to the total system, as the Russians recognised, control can be centralised while local units become semi-autonomous. The feedback loops enable the centre to know about and react to serious deviations or problems at a local level immediately. The result is that control is intensified, while the local unit (factory or whatever) genuinely experiences greater freedom of decision-making.

In Etzioni's theory of societal guidance, the central concepts of cybernetics (control, information, feedback, neg-entropy, homeostasis) form the basis of day-to-day social organisation and functioning, and are distinguished from the technological base of cybernetics (computers and automated machinery), which are used to explain the genesis of social change. Because social change is regarded as inevitable, for Etzioni the central question is how to control change so that the transformation of society occurs ually. He argues that while no society has significantly altered its power base and stratification structure without a revolution, Western societies did gradually, yet radically, transform themselves once with the move from feudalism to capitalism, and it is therefore conceivable that this process could be repeated. The distinction for Etzioni is not between revolution and reform, but between revolution and 'transforming' reform on the one hand and 'bit' reform on the other. The problem of action is how to achieve a state of 'permanent revolution' without sudden, violent starts and stops, and without fundamentally jeopardising the capitalist economic and democratic order.[34]

He argues that a second major transformation of society is already occurring and can be seen in the expanding welfare state, governmental guidance of the economy and other societal processes, and the mobilisation of relatively powerless groups in the political process. But in Etzioni's view the society itself is experiencing a lag between the introduction of the new science and technology and its social adaptation to them.[35] The only positive choice he sees for society in the 'post modern' period is to achieve fully the 'active society'. This is the society of the future, the guided society, where there is both a higher level of consensus and control. Britain, for instance, is described as a partially-guided society, closer today to the ideal than, for instance, the United States. But change is too slow, as the many pressure groups officially and unofficially brought into the process of legislation and administration so extend the time taken to make a decision that by the time it is achieved the character of the problem has often substantially changed.[36]

Technology and social change

The origin of this major transformation of society is technology; thus like Lenin, who argued that socialism plus electrification equals communism, Etzioni argues that liberal democracy plus cybernetification equals the active society. Etzioni's theory of change is thus materialist, but he attempts to refute, rather than develop, Marx by claiming that history is propelled, not by class struggle, but by struggles internal to each group 'to mobilise under given conditions for the purpose of changing them'. Thus, for Etzioni, the divide is between the mobilised and unmobilised in one and the same collectivity or society.

Participation

Because Etzioni regards mobilisation, or participation, as central in achieving the ideal of the active society, he recognises that extensive changes in the organisation of societal decision-making are essential. Contemporary political decision-making is, by and large, obsolete as it cannot and does not build an adequate consensus which is crucial for a stable society. This criticism of the contemporary democratic process is shared for very different reasons by a variety of analysts and commentators, two of whom, C. B. Macpherson and Carola Pateman, whose work has been widely discussed, we will briefly examine here.[37]

All three, Etzioni, Macpherson and Pateman criticise the conventional theory of liberal democracy which has held sway since Joseph Schumpeter's *Capitalism, Socialism and Democracy* was published in 1943. Schumpeter and, later, Robert Dahl, propounded an empirically grounded theory of democracy which broke with the classical conception by emphasising the social stability of minimal citizen participation—preferably by intermittently—and not too vigorously—expressing their choice between alternative elites through the ballot-box. In their view, excessive participation is dangerous and savours of totalitarianism. At the core of this model of democracy, apathy=stability.

Macpherson regards this variant of democracy as very limited, in that it regards the citizen only as a 'consumer' and not as a 'doer'; a criticism very much shared by Pateman. Her particular interest in people 'doing' or working, as against consuming, leads her to examine the possibility of greater participation in the work situation. Pateman, like Etzioni, acknowledges that any significant increase in participation requires institutional change. This is easily distinguished from the all too common situation where a central department or local authority talks of participation but has simply failed to spell out the power to be allocated at the periphery and its relationship to the power to be kept by the centre. In such a situation, participation is tokenistic, and very much the bottom rung of Sherry Arnstein's 'ladder of participation', or 'pseudo' in Pateman's language.[38] In the event it is clear that the elite is unresponsive in that it can offer only the opportunity to say 'yes' to its proposals. Participation is thus a process of cooling-in people to decisions which have in fact been taken in advance, and which, apart from small, even derisory points, will not be changed.

The perspective from which Macpherson and Pateman criticise the empiricists is thus not merely that their conception of democracy is inadequate, but that in a society freed from necessity a theory of democracy should be about more than the registering of consumer preferences; it should provide a framework within which people can develop their essentially human qualities. Macpherson is particularly ascerbic in his criticism of both Schumpeter and Dahl, arguing that their claims to scientificity are based on the crude and far from neutral belief that 'whatever works is right.' Etzioni equally opposes the minimum participation theory, not on openly philosophical grounds, but on pragmatic grounds, namely that minimum participation does *not* work, as it neither can nor does achieve an adequate consensus. If we contrast the mechanistic Etzioni with the humanistic Pateman and Macpherson, we see that while Macpherson and Pateman want a better society, Etzioni merely wants one which works better.

Etzioni identifies two groups whose participation must be encouraged in order to achieve the active society: 'lower participants' and 'elites'. The present society he describes as 'inauthentic' which 'hides from its own elites as well as from observers the extent to which consensus has been lost'. Inauthenticity arises from manipulation in the broadest sense, in that it provides the appearance of being responsive to the needs of individuals while the underlying condition is, in fact, alienating. Those with little or no voice in decision-making affect societal action, if only by their passive resistance or disaffection. But these groups are difficult to mobilise; their consciousness is at a low level, as they tend to accept the prevailing view of society and share its 'consumption obsession, mass culture and apolitical deflection'. Because of their inauthentic involvement, their objective condition is more hidden than when they were simply alienated as in the first period of industrialisation. By including inauthentically involved, and therefore in reality excluded, groups in the political process, both social control and genuine consensus are increased. This theory is widely shared, if not expressed, among community workers and activists, and a number of action projects illustrate attempts to affect the behaviour of previously socially excluded groups through participation in community activities of various kinds.[39]

To become active, a society must overcome another major problem—the unresponsiveness of elites. Elites that do not respond to 'lower participants' may be contributing to a future explosive situation, a point *Realpolitik* has long recognised.[40] It is an awareness of this that may lead the powerful to allow underprivileged groups to participate in political decision-making. The hope is that their participation will drain, rather than increase, their efforts to change society fundamentally. But Etzioni also argues that in the active society, given the increase in material affluence and the effect of liberal arts education, elites are less concerned with the acquisition of material goods and consumption and place more value on social usefulness as a basis for action. Thus elites are said to be prepared to give up some of their material advantage in exchange for symbolic rewards.

To the extent that this is so, consensus-building is facilitated, as while material scarcity is inevitable there is no such limit to participation in cultural and political activities. He says that although an increased number of participants will lengthen the time it takes to reach a consensus, when achieved it will be all the more mobilising because of the time and effort involved. Thus all citizens can have their expressive needs met and be rewarded symbolically through a process of absorbing their energies, 'in particular their political energies through institutionalised (though not bureaucratic) structures'.

A cybernetic model

Etzioni wishes to replace the apathy/stability model of society with its antithesis, a model of activity/stability. Thus planners who, in the name of participation, presently seek to adjust the planned to decisions already taken are merely increasing inauthenticity, as they have failed to recognise the importance of mobilising different collectivities and through inter-conflict achieve a new active consensus. Further, rationalistic planning is rejected as inadequate as the amount of power required to implement any master design is considerable, given the resistance and alienation this method generates.

To achieve a society which works better and avoids widespread alienation means that new ways must be found to introduce consensus-building into the process of government. This is a pressing problem, as agencies traditionally engaged in consensus-building and, to a lesser extent, control are weakening. What we are experiencing is a decline in the power of legislatures in favour of their executives, and within these executives an increase in the power and role of experts. This process is occurring in part because of the massive growth of the information industry, the output of which is monopolised largely by the executive, which presents findings selectively to the legislature. In addition, legislatures are composed of regional representatives, while planning and action units are either functional or trans-regional.

The reorganised Health Service in Britain exemplifies this process. Information flows are central to the new structure, and relate to functional divisions of medical care. While the actual geographical units correspond to the new local authority areas, function is split from representation and the service is to be managed by experts drawn from administration and the medical professions. The new structure thus consolidates and rationalises trends in administration of health which have been becoming increasingly clear over recent years.[41]

Although the new model is semi-cybernetic in that it focuses on information, the information-gathering process is entirely mechanistic and fails to involve more than the medical elites. In terms of a cybernetic theory, the organisation of the NHS is obsolescent in that, having further moved away from control by traditional democratic procedures, it has devised no new procedures to include the other Health Service participants and general public. It thus falls between the past and the present/future.

While recognising that, in the short run, mobilisation of collectivities will increase conflict, given an 'interwoven' approach and a society that is reasonably well integrated, the conflict, Etzioni says, will not lead to breakdown but to a new consensus. In this fully cybernetic model the perspective of the formally recognised decision-makers and those likely to be affected by the plan are taken into account in a structure where the decision-making and planning units are less segregated than is usual at present. There are two distinctive features: the inclusion in one group of both the planners and the representatives of the groups whose activities are to be regulated, while the initial plans are neither detailed nor prescriptive but provide a context. Clearly, the model of 'contextuating state control', combined with delegation of 'bit control' to a plurality of member organisations, enables greater participation to take place and thus social control is more closely linked to the formation of consensus.

This, then, is the ideal 'conflict-limiting capsule' or organisation or a participating society. The parties lose some of their elf-sufficiency by being tied into the society and some of their autonomy by being subject to a shared political organisation. In cybernetic terms, both the controller and the controlled are linked reciprocally through feedback loops. Thus relationships hitherto characterised by domination move towards reciprocity.[42]

Donnison, in his proposal for a new local organisational pattern for deprived areas, suggests a practical scheme that is very similar to Etzioni's theoretical model.[43] He sees the need to create more sophisticated 'meshes' of the political and bureaucratic systems along with a more effective means of arbitration. The new combination must be fashioned at a micro-political level in order to incorporate three elements: 1. more and better services, 2. better opportunities for local people to seek and make their demands heard, and 3. the creation of unseen alliances between the deprived and sympathetic professionals to secure more resources. This potential support from the professionals becomes overt when the deprived have mobilised public opinion to their cause. In Etzioni's terms, lower participants would be mobilised and elites enabled to become more socially responsive.

The actual structure to accomplish these aims would consist of decentralised local service centres providing a multitude of services such as citizens' advice, housing and rent officers, social services—including intensive family casework, education, probation, maternity and child welfare. They would also be given enlarged decision-making powers, with the area officer being compared to a 'company commander' generally responsible for his area of the 'front'. This analogy conveys the flavour not of the man in the middle between two opposing camps, but that of the front man for one side—the elite—meeting the enemy on the other—the lower participants. The latter would be organised through neighbourhood councils and every effort would be made to encourage the survival of grassroots organisations. For instance, local groups would be given financial support, perhaps through some independent body like the existing research councils or the university grants committee, as these are less exposed to local political pressure.

The aims of the scheme would be to enable greater decentralisation of governmental powers to take place, yet result in greater co-ordination between community-based initiatives of various kinds and the existing political and administrative structures of local and national government. Looked at in terms of cybernetic

READ.

theory and the existing use of community workers, the feedback loop becomes much more elaborate than a single community worker liaising between the statutory authority and community groups.

While Donnison says these measures would not eliminate social conflict and the threat of urban guerilla warfare, the aims would be to promote 'productive conflict' and 'furnish procedures for successive temporary arbitrations and agreements'. He claims that the services people need in an urban area do not involve them in 'zero sum games' where every win is someone else's loss, but rather that needs such as housing, play-space, jobs, welfare services, can be extended, subdivided and redistributed 'almost indefinitely'. This makes arbitration feasible, 'because everyone can gain something from it'.

Looked at in terms of the community worker's or activist's role in creating and maintaining such systems of information flow and arbitration, the crucial question to be asked of Donnison is whether the management of resources is a zero sum game or not. No matter how clever the structure, can the existing political and economic system convert the existing scramble for scarce resources like housing into a genuine redistribution—or will the 'endless subdivisions' created by endless alterations of administration do no more than draw a veil over a zero sum game?

Co-option, encapsulation and pacification

Most community workers and activists are conscious of the problem of co-option. What Etzioni usefully does is to distinguish between co-option, by which he means the recruitment of individual activists, and encapsulation, by which he means capturing the organisation or even social movement. Encapsulation thus institutionalises conflict, transforming its nature by self-imposed rules of conduct.[44] To the extent that the participants limit their modes of strife without any influence or force being exerted by the larger society or some segment of it, encapsulation is self-propelling. Once encapsulated, the collectivity loses some of its self-sufficiency by being tied into the larger society, and some of its autonomy by being subject to the same political organisation.

If conflict cannot be managed by the process of encapsulation, then the only means left to the elites is that of pacification, as discussed by Kitson,[45] and exemplified by the role of the British Army in Northern Ireland. Etzioni regards this as an inferior strategy as it requires more energy and resources, is more difficult to achieve, and produces a temporary rather than permanent quiescence to the conflict. What becomes important sociologically is to locate the capsule, that is, the organisational forms by which the authorities are to encapsulate the mobilised collectivities. In the last analysis, Etzioni's theoretical model, like Donnison's practical one, takes a very mechanistic view of organisation. While social responsiveness is basic to both, neither seems to take this really seriously. Even if 'lower participants' could be successfully organised, it is unlikely that 'elites' would make sufficient resources available to solve key social problems. Both models essentially share a platonic view of the elite—their philosopher-kings are the new technocrats—and suggest a harmonious order which glosses over the profound class antagonisms that divide society.

Thus Donnison's plan leaves out what happens when the 'local service centres' cannot, or will not, deliver the goods. This model fails to account for the kind of situation exemplified by the long struggle to secure the rights of homeless people. Since 1961 there has been an extended campaign mounted by pressure and activist groups to compel local authorities to fulfil their statutory duty to the homeless. When success appears to be in sight, then the rules of the game are altered by a calculatedly 'unresponsive' elite, and the local authority has permissive powers at present rather than a duty. In so far as the theory of the cybernetic society requires that elites be responsive, it appears to need a better reason than either Etzioni or Donnison provides for their enlightened conduct.

For that matter, basic differences in perception and interest between individuals and groups involved in community action projects make their agreement to join, and systematically work through, neighbourhood councils unlikely. People can be relatively easily mobilised over a relevant issue, but the experience of long-term participation in such groups is not encouraging.[46]

Participation and change

None the less, despite the weaknesses in the theory of the cybernetic democracy, important questions are raised at the strategic level for community organising, whether carried out as part of community work practice or as an informal activity. Community organising can be evaluated in a variety of ways. It is clear, for example, that people profoundly stigmatised for their poverty, their race or gender, by organising themselves, and learning to struggle collectively for social justice, can in fact de-label themselves.[47] Yet in the actual practice of community organising, the interaction between theory and practice is continuous while at the level of the individual it is likely to appear inconsistent. What, therefore, we are concerned with is the strategic level, not with the individual, but with the collectivity.

The question—to use Etzioni's terms—is not whether the individual is co-opted but whether the collectivity is encapsulated. Put concretely, the question is not, as it was very widely formulated, have Jim Radford and Ron Bailey sold out—but whether squatting as a collective activity has become encapsulated? While the two may be connected, it is not a necessary connection, and a leadership may retain its radical rhetoric but none the less experience encapsulation.

In principle, forms of community organising, work and development are likely to be encouraged in areas with acute social problems where the existing political systems are unable to respond, or in areas where they do not exist. Thus, in situations where there is little democracy, as in New Towns or various colonial and neo-colonial situations, community development is strong and taken for granted. The cybernetic democracy, with its apparent participation at the grass roots and control through information at the top, facilitates the weakening of our present forms of liberal democracy. Thus when community workers and activists help to create the cybernetic model of social functioning, they may be using participation as a substitute for a real redistribution of resources. It may be that participation is the one limitless resource contemporary society is prepared to offer the 'lower participant'.

Last, if Hindess's thesis concerning the change in the Labour Party so that it is less an expression of working-class policies than those of the radical middle classes is correct, this process is likely to be facilitated rather than hindered by the formal democratic structure.[48] Lacking personal experience of the working-class situation, the new-style Labour councillors will need survey data and information derived from participatory exercises, in a way that the traditional Labour councillors did not. In their attempt to secure the necessary knowledge for them to discharge their responsibility, particularly that they feel towards the most pressed of their working-class electorate, they are encouraging forms of community participation which could potentially render the role of the local councillor obsolete. The low turn-out at elections has for some time

roduced questions concerning the legitimacy of the local
ouncillors. Now the growth of micro-politics or community action,
ncouraged by new-style councillors, threatens that participation, as
. social technology may well be associated with social change—not
owards a participatory democracy, but towards a cybernetic
ociety.

Notes

1 H. Rose, 'Up against the welfare state: the claimant unions', in R. Miliband
   and J. Saville (eds), *The Socialist Register 1973,* Merlin, 1974, pp. 179–203;
   R. Bailey, *The Squatters,* Penguin, 1973; N. Dennis, *Public Participation and
   Planner's Blight,* Faber & Faber, 1972.

2 See for example: T. B. Bottomore, *Sociology, a Guide to Problems and
   Literature,* rev. ed. Allen & Unwin, 1971, pp. 15–47; R. Aron, *German
   Sociology,* Collier-Macmillan, 1965; A. Gouldner, *The Coming Crisis of
   Western Sociology,* Heinemann, 1971; R. Nisbet, *The Sociological Tradition,*
   Heinemann, 1967, pp. 3–20.

3 R. Nisbet, 'Sociology as an art form', in M. Stein and A. Vidich (eds),
   Sociology on Trial, Spectrum Books, 1963, pp. 147–66; incidentally the
   same year as John Madge published *The Origins of Scientific Sociology*
   (Tavistock, 1963), hailing the Lynds' Middletown study as objective.

4 Gouldner (op. cit.) points out the fit between Comte's marginality as an
   aristocrat, his positivistic commitment and this mix of ideas.

5 Nisbet (1963), p. 349; J. Horton makes a very similar point for the central
   Marxian conception of alienation: 'Contemporary definitions of anomie and
   alienation have confused, obscured, and changed the classical meanings of
   these concepts . . . The concepts imply complete social theories explaining
   relationships between a social condition and behaviour. Critical concepts,
   they also imply the judgment of society in terms of ideal, or at least future
   and unrealized standards . . . Today de-humanization has set in, the concepts
   have been transmogrified into things instead of evaluations about things, and
   it is no longer clear what alienated men are alienated from.' ('The
   de-humanization of anomie and alienation: a problem in the ideology of
   sociology', *British Journal of Sociology,* 15 (4), 1964, pp. 283–300), also
   'The fetishism of sociology', in J. D. Colfax and J. L. Roach (eds), *Radical
   Sociology,* Basic Books, 1971, pp. 171–93.

6 'These small stereotyped forms [the traditional Indian village] of social
   organism have been to the greater part disappearing, not so much through the
   brutal interference of the British tax gatherer and the British soldier as
   through the workings of English steam and English trade . . . Now sickening
   as it must be to human feeling to witness these myriads of industrious
   patriarchal and inoffensive social organisations disorganised and dissolved
   into their units thrown into a sea of woes, and their hereditary means of
   subsistence, we must not forget that these idyllic village communities,
   inoffensive though they may appear, had always been the solid foundation of

Oriental despotism, that they restrained the human mind within the smalles
compass, making it the unresisting tool of superstition, enslaving it beneath
traditional rules, depriving it of all grandeur and historical energies.' (K
Marx, 'The British rule in India', *New York Tribune*, 1951, reprinted in L. S
Feuer (ed.), *Marx and Engels: Basic Writings on Politics and Philosophy*
Fontana, 1969, p. 517.) On religion, Marx writes: 'Religion is at the same
time the expression of real distress and the protest against real distress
Religion is the sigh of the oppressed creature, the heart of a heartless world,
just as it is the spirit of an unspiritual situation. It is the opium of the
people . . . The abolition of religion as the *illusory* happiness of the people is
required for their *real* happiness.' ('Toward the critique of Hegel's
philosophy of right', in Feuer (op. cit.), p. 303.)

7 Nisbet argues: 'Sociology, more than any other scholarly discipline, has taken the conflicts between traditionalism and modernism in European culture and converted them into a set of analytical concepts . . . We live in a late phase of the classical age of sociology. Strip from present day sociology the perspectives and frameworks provided by men like Weber and Durkheim and little would be left but lifeless heaps of data and stray hypotheses.' (*The Sociological Tradition*, p.viii.)

8 P. and P. Goodman, *Communitas*, N.Y., Vintage Books, 1966; P. Kropotkin, *Fields, Factories and Workshops*, Sonnenschein (Swan), 1901; and *Memoirs of a Revolutionist*, Sonnenschein (Swan), 1906 (Dover, 1971).

9 C. Bell and H. Newby quote approvingly Ruth Glass's denunciation of the nostalgia embedded in community studies: 'The poor sociologist's substitute for the novel'. They criticise as she does that non-cumulative nature of the work, its statistical weakness. Their definition of a community study is very close to that proposed by Stacey. But what is most striking about the book is its intense claim to scientificity; thus the authors conclude: 'One final word on the avoidance of normative prescription in community studies. The authors of this book are as keen as any on the good life. We also have some pretty clear ideas as to what it consists of. But we felt that it would be unreasonable, not to say dangerous, if we were to foist our normative prescriptions on unsuspecting readers, especially if they were masquerading as sociology'. (*Community Studies: An Introduction to the Sociology of the Local Community*, Allen & Unwin, 1972, p. 252.)

10 R.J. Havighurst and A.J. Jensen, 'Community research', *Current Sociology*, 15 (2), 1967, regard community research as a form of research, not an area of sociology. A. Vidich, J. Bensman and M.R. Stein, *Reflections on Community Studies*, Wiley, 1964; G. Hillery, 'Definitions of community: areas of agreement', *Rural Sociology*, 20 (2), 1955, pp. 111-23.

11 The presence of 'people' in the concept of community should not be as lightly dismissed as scientific sociology tends to do; instead, as Horton points out for 'alienation', the concept is *dehumanised* and is instead *reified* into locality and network.

12 Margaret Stacey, 'The myth of community studies', *British Journal of Sociology*, 20 (2), 1969, pp. 134-47; Jacqueline Scherer, *Contemporary Community: Sociological Illusion or Reality*, Tavistock, 1972; Maurice Stein, *The Eclipse of Community*, N.Y., Harper Torchbooks, 1964.

3 Margaret Stacey, *Tradition and Change: A Study of Banbury*, Oxford University Press, 1960.

4 For example, P. Selznick has, according to Wolin, an organicist theory of organisations. Terms such as spontaneity, natural process, adaptive organisms, non-rational behaviour, are used not to describe a rural pre-industrial society but General Motors, the Pentagon and large universities: S. Wolin, in A. Etzioni (ed.), *A Sociological Reader on Complex Organisations*, N.Y., Holt, Rinehart & Winston, 1969.

5 R. Glass, 'Urban sociology in Great Britain: a trend report', *Current Sociology*, 4 (4), 1955; 'Conflict in cities', in A. V. S. de Reuck and J. Knight (eds), *Conflict in Society*, Churchill, 1966, pp. 141-62.

6 R. Pahl, 'The rural urban continuum', in R. Pahl (ed.), *Readings in Urban Sociology*, Pergamon, 1968, pp. 263-305; H. Gans, *The Urban Villagers*, N.Y., Free Press, 1962.

7 R. Frankenberg, *Communities in Britain*, Penguin, 1966; C. Bell and H. Newby, op. cit.; R. Pahl, *Patterns of Urban Life*, Longman, 1970.

8 J. Barnes, 'Class and committees in a Norwegian island parish', *Human Relations*, 7 (1), 1954, pp. 39-58; E. Bott, *Family and Social Network*, Tavistock, 1957; J. C. Mitchell (ed.), *Social Networks in Urban Situations*, Manchester University Press, 1969.

9 The divorce between the home and the workplace has created all sorts of problems for sociology; thus we have the irony of Stacey referring to community studies as being of non-work relations, yet what the woman does is clearly a form of work, albeit indirectly locked into the productive process. It is fascinating, sociologically, that the care of children when paid is regarded as work and not when not paid. Bell and Newby, despite the importance of family as a component within community, actually define out family as being beyond their concern, thus the Institute of Community Studies' work is—for them—about family, not community. Work both in and outside the home is linked by N. Dennis, L. F. Henriques and C. Slaughter's book *Coal is our Life*, Eyre & Spottiswoode, 1956—the chapter on family being particularly interesting in this respect.

20 One such critique of the position of women developed from a Marxist perspective is that of S. James and M. Dalla Costa, *The Power of Women and the Subversion of the Community*, Bristol, Falling Wall Press, 1972.

21 A. R. Radcliffe-Brown, *A Natural Science of Society*, Chicago, Free Press, 1957, remains the most frank exposition of this standpoint.

22 Gouldner, op. cit.; M. Nicolaus, 'The professional organisation of sociology, a view from below', *Antioch Review*, 29 (3), reprinted in J. D. Colfax and J. L. Roach (eds), *Radical Sociology*, pp. 45-60, and R. Blackburn (ed.), *Ideology in Social Science*, Fontana, 1972, pp. 45-60.

23 This was the code-name for an extensively funded research programme into social change in Latin America, which was exposed as a counter-insurgency programme financed by the CIA: I. L. Horowitz (ed.), *The Rise and Fall of Project Camelot*, Massachusetts Institute of Technology Press, 1967.

24 T. S. Kuhn, *The Structure of Scientific Revolutions*, University of Chicago Press, 1962. There is, however, a growing critique of the objectivity of natural science which has since the Lysencko affair remained unquestioned.

See H. Rose and S. Rose, 'The radicalisation of science', in R. Miliband and J. Saville (eds), *The Socialist Register 1972*, Merlin, pp. 105-32.

25 Several of the papers in R. Whitley (ed.), *Social Processes in Scientific Development*, Routledge & Kegan Paul, 1974, point to this new direction.

26 There is a return to the analysis opened in 1931 by B. Hessen, a Soviet Marxist physicist, in N. Bukharin, *Science at the Crossroads*, 1931, reprinted by Cass, 1971; G. Böhme, W. Daele and W. Krohn, 'Alternativen in der Wissenschaft', *Zeitschrift für Soziologie*, 1 (4), 1972; also H. Rose and S. Rose (eds), *Ideology in Natural Science*, Penguin (in press).

27 T. Roszak, *The Making of a Counter-Culture*, Faber & Faber, 1970.

28 Increasingly the work of the Frankfurt School is becoming available in English, such as the key writings of Adorno, Marcuse, Habermas, Horkheimer. More recently A. Schmidt's work, *The Concept of Nature and Marx*, New Left Books, 1974; and W. Leiss, *The Domination of Nature*, N.Y., Braziller, 1972, have been published. M. Jay, *The Dialectical Imagination* Heinemann, 1973, provides a good account of the goods and achievements of the School.

29 J. Ellul, *The Technological Society*, Vintage Books, 1967.

30 A. Etzioni, *The Active Society*, Collier-Macmillan, 1968.

31 D. V. Donnison *et al.*, *London: Urban Patterns, Problems and Policies*, Heinemann, 1973, pp. 383-404.

32 Cybernation has affected work in a number of ways, by displacing the unskilled, creating an even greater distance between the individual and the product of his work, and increasing the importance of leisure. One unplanned social impact of the new technology is to contribute to the ability of individuals to reverse sex roles; in particular more service type occupations give men more opportunity to perform aspects of the traditional feminine role: R. Perrucci and M. Pilisuk (eds), *The Triple Revolution Emerging*, Boston, Little, Brown, 1971.

33 An interesting debate between John Adams and Stafford Beer illuminates some of the problems of a cybernetic social theory; John Adams, 'Everything under control', *Science for People*, no. 21, April-May 1973, pp. 4-6; Stafford Beer, 'You evince no cybernetic consciousness', *Science for People*, no. 22, June-July 1973, pp. 5-6.

34 It would not be too much of an overstatement to suggest that Etzioni sees himself as a Mao or a Trotsky of the West. However what we will have to discuss in a subsequent paper is the implication of Christopher Zeeman's 'catastrophe theory', which specifies the conditions under which cybernetic systems break down.

35 W. F. Ogburn, *Social Change: With Respect to Culture and Original Nature*, N.Y., Heubsch, 1922, developed the concept of 'cultural lag' to describe those situations where changes in the non-material culture do not keep pace with those of the material. Social stress and conflict result from their not being synchronised with each other.

36 S. H. Beer, *Modern British Politics: A Study of Parties and Pressure Groups*, Faber & Faber, 1965; N. Annan, 'This unhappy breed', *New York Review of Books*, 5 (7), 1965, pp. 25-8.

7 C. B. Macpherson, *Democratic Theory: Essays in Retrieval,* Oxford University Press, London, 1973; C. Pateman, *Participation and Democratic Theory,* Oxford University Press, 1971. The same concern is expressed by C. G. Benello, 'Participatory democracy and the dilemma of change', in P. Long (ed.), *The New Left,* Boston, Sargent, 1969, pp. 404–19.

8 S. Arnstein, 'A ladder of participation', *Journal of the American Institute of Planners,* 35 (4), 1969, pp. 216–24; a similar view is expressed in H. Rose and T. Puckett, 'Blue prints for bureaucrats', *Journal of the Royal Institute of British Architects,* no. 6, June 1973, pp. 273–81.

9 G. Braeger discusses how to organise citizen involvement in order to heighten community integration in the Organising the Unaffiliated programme of Mobilisation for Youth. The fundamental tactic was co-option of local leaders by hiring them as part-time organisers and of indigenous organisations by providing them with services. The problem for sponsors and organisers was to avoid the upwardly mobile individual who is not representative of his community and already, by virtue of his ambition, isolated from it: 'Organising the unaffiliated in a low-income area', in A. Etzioni (ed.), *A Sociological Reader on Complex Organisations.*

40 From Machiavelli to Quintin Hogg in 1945—'we must reform or be reformed'—elites have always seen the necessity of flexibility in the face of serious popular pressure.

41 See P. Draper and T. Smart, *Social Science and Health Policy in the U.K.* (forthcoming), for an analysis of the philosophy of scientific management which underlies both the structure of the new NHS and also its associated research.

42 This essentially is the argument of B.F. Skinner in *Beyond Freedom and Dignity,* Cape, 1972.

43 Donnison, op. cit.

44 Etzioni elaborates his discussion of encapsulation as a historical process both within one country, e.g. labour management relations in the US, but also between countries, e.g. east-west détente: *Studies in Social Change,* Holt, Rinehart & Winston, 1967.

45 F. Kitson, *Low Intensity Operations,* Faber & Faber, 1971.

46 This fragility of community groups as against the persistence of most trade unions has been extensively reported by research; certainly we have also found this both in our USA and our UK work.

47 See, for example, H. Rose, 'Who can de-label the claimant?', *Social Work Today,* 4 (13), 1973, pp. 409–13.

48 B. Hindess, *The Decline of Working-Class Politics,* Paladin, 1971.

3 Politics, theory and community work

Laurence Tasker

In the debate surrounding the question of a definition or delimitation of community work there is growing attention to the common concerns and identity of practice in community work and adult education. 'Social work' as a definition has not proved helpful or informative. The popular reference to community work as 'a method of social work' presupposes a definition of social work itself, and this remains elusive. Casework, which represents conceptually the best understood—and practically the most representative—form of social work, compares at few points, and certainly not at its most fundamental, with community work. Thus, there is, essentially no 'casework relationship' in community work. Those with whom the worker is in contact personally are not those to whom the purpose of his work is ultimately directed, and this radically alters the quality of the relationships the worker makes. Furthermore, there is little intellectual grounding in common between the two practices and, generally, emotional imperatives are quite different (and in reverse order of importance to intellectual reasons for undertaking the job) between the two types of worker. In community work, moreover, a key concept in social work is frequently quite absent: the notion of care, though this can be a payoff of a community development programme and might even form a specialism within the profession.

On a positive note, the two jobs share the role of advocacy, a point of contact which one hopes will be developed. However this is an aspect which *characterises* neither. Typically, moreover, the community worker is not concerned with crisis resolution, which is a central concern of social work. The 'problems' he defines often would not be described thus by the community itself. He is aiming to increase choice and develop abilities to take advantage of choice, with an aim of improving the quality of life—often where no agreed condition of pathology prevails. But he is not simply by nature a 'resource-person'. He will hopefully be able to achieve such a

46

unction. However, describing his practice thus and therefore ttributing to it the status 'non-directive' is as discredited among ommunity workers as would be a claim to 'objectivity' in social cience. The partiality of his intervention is recognised as inherent, nd must be embraced in the concept of the community worker's ask. The aim of this task is an increased ability to act ollectively—this objective to be achieved through a process of ducation and self-education instigated by the community worker. such day-to-day activities as advocacy may in practice occupy a high proportion of the community worker's time, but this is not what haracterises his work. He is not treating emotional or material rises; he is engendering the ability—where this did not exist before—to take measures towards an increase in the quality of life hrough collective action. This is the function of an educator, and is he role in which the community worker's contributions and esponsibilities may be most successfully understood. For the purposes of this discussion it is important to consider what relation he development in question and the role played by the community vorker have to the processes of political life.

Introducing the concept of 'politics' leads us to a second problem of definition. Constitution, international relations and voting behaviour are some of the many sub-fields of political science, and he endeavour to ascertain what is common to these is, understandably, problematic. One of the most satisfactory for our purposes, however, comes from the literature of community work tself. In describing the objectives of community work (or community organisation' in the author's American usage), Murray Ross[1] says the community 'identifies its needs or objectives, orders or ranks) these needs or objectives, develops the confidence and will o work at these needs and objectives, finds the resources (internal und/or external) to deal with these needs or objectives, takes action n respect to them, and in so doing extends and develops cooperative und collaborative attitudes and practices in the community.' While he same criticism of this statement—that it takes no, or too little, account of conflict processes in groups—would be levelled by the political scientist as by the community worker, it otherwise stands as un acceptable statement of the fundamental process of political life. t is of course a description of community work itself.

The ability—or the fact—of acting together is, to the political scientist, the essence of political life. Thus in an analytical sense the *objective to be achieved* in the process of community development is a political development introduced by the community worker in the community in question. The extent to which this has any consequence for professional practice or in the real world of politic must now be considered.

The analytical statement above would be thought irrelevant by many community workers, particularly those anxious to assert the neutrality of their positions in a political sense. Indeed it is a question more likely to preoccupy the political scientist than the community development worker. There are, however, two important reasons for making the point. First, it must be recognised that successful development in a neighbourhood (or whatever other grouping is being described as a 'community') of a capability among the populace to act collectively, although in the short term viewed a successful but not politically relevant community development must be considered in the long term for secondary—political—effect on the community concerned. For example the self-confidence arising from such a scheme as street wardenship, a community newspaper, a community association or other ostensibly apolitical body is likely to give a very different spirit to the community in situation where common interests are threatened. Thus skill required in organising street parties are not very dissimilar from those needed in staging a rent strike. Forming a community association involves similar organisation to electing tenants representatives to a local council.

Such political acts on the part of a local community often will no occur for the reason, simply, that there is no precedent in the community to give the necessary confidence or any of the basic experience and abilities for such ideas to appear viable. The experience of successful community development projects, however, brings the community appreciably nearer to these capabilities. Inspiration need not come directly from the community worker. A community which 'orders and deals with its problems' cannot be expected not to act as its own advocate when the occasion arises. In short, the population who, through the efforts of the worker, have in some sense become a community in themselves, are likely—in paraphrasing a former theorist of political change—to become a community for themselves.

We are here of course speaking of a tendency, and it is clear that neither the success nor duration of such community work as that implicit in these examples will be typical of all projects in either voluntary or statutory fields. But inherently the tendency is there, and the claim by a community worker that his professional practice is 'non-political' is not acceptable. It may not be politically motivated in the partisan or ideological sense, but its political character is fundamental and its potential significance in everyday politics cannot be ignored A claim by a worker, therefore, to choose to devote himself to other aspects of his professional task and deny the need for some political sophistication on his own part must be deemed naive or irresponsible. In terms of the basic nature of political life as described conceptually above, and in terms of intervention in conventional political processes the community worker is playing a contributory role, and his professionalism requires him to acknowledge and accommodate to this.

The purpose of the foregoing discussion is not to stress political to the exclusion of other intrinsic benefits of community development work. Recreation, environmental improvement and communication are all possible products of community development which are valuable in their own right. It is the reluctance of many workers, and more especially of their employers, to acknowledge a political aspect which is the second reason for emphasising this point. It is a pity that the meaning of 'political' in everyday parlance has become so restricted and so pejorative. In most people's minds the word tends to equal 'partisan', and therefore is synonymous with the notion of conflict. To behave politically, in such a conception, is to take the part of some contestant in the regular political process—in general a party or well recognised pressure-group, or personally joining battle in the day-to-day political scene. A group or community taking a decision or acting together—albeit peacefully—does not, alas, form part of the popular concept of the political.

Moreover, there is an unfortunate tradition that anything so designated is to be condemned as unacceptable according to the normal bounds of propriety. 'Politics' equals 'dirty'. But the pursuit of their common interests by a group, though it may not be partisan, is political. Why encouragement of such a group by a community worker should not be applauded is inexcusable. Unfortunately, the concept makes directors in both statutory and voluntary agencies nervous, thus often bringing them into conflict with the basic aims of their organisations. In the local government sphere, reports affecting policy in three departments have recently stressed organisation of the public as consumers of services; namely Skeffington, Seebohm and Russell. And in relation to under-privileged groups, such an attitude must be viewed as particularly unreasonable. Apart from its relationship to material benefit and prosperity, political expression is a fundamental to human fulfilment and dignity. This is well recognised in the constitution of this country. Yet, in the last hundred or so years, during a period of unparalleled change in other dimensions of life, this aspect has remained basically static.

Community workers have little in their training to give them a more sophisticated political awareness—in relation to either constitutional or theoretical aspects. Those whose background is basically in the field of social work are unlikely to have experience in politics as an academic subject for few social work courses in this country include the subject as either an optional or compulsory part of the curriculum. In fact, in the training situation, social workers are often specifically discouraged from developing strong 'political'* interests, as this is held to be contrary to the ethos of the profession. Among employers, social services and education directors are vehemently, often obsessively, anti-political and would express horror at the suggestion that their employees should encourage something described as a 'political potential' among their client groups. Yet this is intrinsically what the objects of community work entail. But self-determination *is* political action. Alas, in voluntary bodies—contrary to the hopes of trainee community workers—the conventional horror of politics can be yet greater than in the statutory sphere.

Politics is defined as a fundamentally suspect activity and beyond the pale of any kind of professional involvement. Though an individual in our community is expected to use his political rights—the means by which he is expected to develop the maturity to take advantage of these remains obscure in administrative attitudes to the matter. The idea of underprivileged sectors of the population achieving advancement and equality *without* greater political sophistication is unrealistic. Yet responsibility for this is not attributed to the social worker and is begrudged to the community worker. It is a paradox that in a country so proud of its democratic institutions there could reign such a derogatory and suspicious attitude towards the notion of the political. This conception that politics is identical with partisanship or discordant social behaviour must be vigorously contested by the community worker and the notion of politics as an aspect of 'community' inherent in the concept of a developed human being—indispensable to his claim to

*Often unspecified, but usually meaning 'partisan' or 'ideological'.

emancipation and equality of opportunity—must be promulgated with the utmost vigour. Only when this understanding is achieved can the nature and integrity of community development processes adequately be understood.

In addition to this miscomprehension there is, however, another which must be criticised from an opposite standpoint; i.e. for a view which over-stresses politics of the conventional sort in its conception of community work. Those who are committed to the profession for expressly political reasons fall roughly into two categories. The first represent an ideological commitment which is developed to the point where the human being is so eclipsed in the conceptual scheme of events as to be effectively subordinated to an overriding notion of historical process. According to such an application of Marxian analysis, Man has relatively little significance as an individual in the short term, and comes of age only after an anticipated and possibly long-term process of social change. This process in theoretical terms is, of course, widely respected, but from the point of view of the practising community worker any view of the individual which presumes to lower his status relative to the interests of a concept or to a historical vision is unacceptable, and evokes the requirement for an ethic—such as that traditionally associated with the 'professions'. Where such views are encountered, though perhaps romantically rather than earnestly professed, they should be treated with great caution.

There are other community workers who have a less structured ideology and base their work on a political commitment of a different kind. This is, broadly, a commitment to the working-class movement. This may be less explicitly expressed; e.g. as a commitment to the 'relief of poverty'. Such approaches are less stigmatised in ideological terms, but are none the less political in character. The commitment is a highly creditable interpretation of priorities in community development if the educational function of the work as described above is recognised. The manually employed, as a social grouping, are—with the possible exception of the elderly—the most underprivileged and least well endowed in terms of skills of co-operation and organisation in the entire community. Providing the approach gives primacy to the interest of the individual in community development strategy, such an approach must be accepted as fully creditable in professional community work, notwithstanding the ideological prejudice it may encounter. Once again, however, caution is required against the romanticism which may apply to such a position, in particular concerning the significance of community work in the overall process of social change. There are very few full-time community workers operating in this country and, even allowing for the training of 'indigenous' leadership, the number is never likely to be high. One community worker may hope to affect significantly communal life among a few thousand people—perhaps 5,000 over three years where his work is very successful—but the working-class of this country comprises, according to any classification, about two-thirds of the population, say 35 million. Among these are probably at least two million[2] constituting the main target group; i.e. those living below the conventional poverty line, and these are geographically well dispersed. Inadequate housing and education extend the severely underprivileged groups even further. But in spite of the concentration of such problems, and although the full population of the working class may not for practical purposes be treated as an underprivileged category, the idea that widespread social change can be instigated on their part by the initiatives of professional community workers is hopelessly unrealistic. The profession is more a phenomenon of social change, not a 'movement' directly causally related to social change. Community workers in isolation must therefore retain some modesty in the overall social significance they ascribe to their own role.

However, the realisation of this prospect need not be taken as a discouragement or viewed as a dismissal of the value of community work in the overall task of political development. Social change on the scale envisaged in the progress of the working-class movement would theoretically have accruing to it large-scale material benefits for the members of the presently underprivileged category. In the vision of the politically committed worker, it is benefits of this nature which figure largest. But it is not necessary to conceive of success in political development only in these terms. Political development takes place at an individual as well as a social level. Although an individual may not benefit from changes following a macro-scale redistribution of resources, he may benefit in both a material and an educational sense from the effects of small-scale change. In the first instance he *is* likely to gain an increase in the material aspects of his own life. These might be the procedure for repair of his house, provision of recreational facilities or implementation of some aspect of welfare policy on a localised basis. Such aspects may seem small and inconsequential to the social-change-oriented community worker. But in condemning the 'insignificance' of such gains, he should not underestimate the immediate significance to such persons to whom traditionally even the most trivial details of social life have been exclusively in the hands of an administrative entity external to his own life and to the community concerned. To an enormous extent, even the smallest benefits of a material nature depend upon the benevolence of an external authority to working-class people. The reversal of this position gives not only a direct benefit to individuals in terms of application of administration more overtly in their interest, but changes the experience of the individual in the new relationship he has to administration and its resources. The experience of politics is not simply the benefits gained from successful campaigning on behalf of some party or group, the payoff of pressure-group activity, or massive social change. The experience of taking part in such a process is as fundamental to humanity as the material payoff which results from it. At the local level this experience is as real as—possibly more real to the individual than—any movement to which he may belong. It is this kind of experience—a 'participatory' experience—which the community worker can hope realistically to introduce at a local level, and it is the notion of political change with which he as an individual worker should feel satisfied, though the reality of the problem of large-scale change remains beyond him.

To return to the broader problem of political change on a national scale. The isolation normal to the community worker is the key to understanding the anomaly of his position in conventional political terms. The client group in such an approach is 'the working-class'—defined in terms of their mode of employment. Yet the workplace typically does not figure at all in the literature of community work or in the typical fieldwork practised by community workers. In a recent meeting with a class of German social work students—most of whom were notably more politically articulate than their British counterparts—I was struck by the dual focus in ideological terms of the pro-working-class cause among them. They were concerned with *Produktions-bereich* and *Reproduktions-bereich*—workplace and dwelling-place or, more literally, 'sphere of production' and 'sphere of reproduction'. These were seen as two foci of working-class cultural deprivation and struggle, and social workers were concerned to ally the efforts they made in the second to those taking place in the first and paramount

area. In British community work this common cause is barel
recognised. One seldom hears the question of a communit
work/trade union link discussed. In a plethora of conferences an
study-groups on community work here over the last few year
hardly a trade union speaker or official delegate has been presen
Whether substantial interest from the trade unions would b
forthcoming remains to be seen, but the community wor
profession can hardly be uninterested in them. They have bee
fighting the working-class cause for over a century, and in a sense sti
have the greatest resources to carry on doing so. If community wor
is to make any contribution to large-scale social change on behalf o
the working-class its best chance will be in co-operation or at least i
dialogue with the movement who has the main experience and ha
played the principal role to date. In this way, meaning and directio
can be given to the pro-working-class efforts in community work
which will otherwise remain a lost cause.

Notes

1 Murray G. Ross and Ben W. Lappin, *Community Organisation—Theory an*
   Principles, 2nd ed., Harper & Row, 1967, p. 40.
2 This estimate is accepted, for example, by J. C. Kincaid in *Poverty an*
   Equality in Britain (Pelican, 1973), though he points out that many estimate
   are far higher.

4 Rehousing in Glasgow: reform through community action*

Sidney Jacobs

Glasgow ranks among the worst housed cities in Western Europe. In spite of the magnitude of its problems, however, it represents the typical rather than the exceptional in Britain, where, to some degree, every local authority suffers from a combination of poor living conditions, housing shortage and bureaucratic administration. Glasgow, although an extreme example, may serve as an illustration of what is generally wrong with housing in Britain; community action in one of the city's clearance areas thus has implications far beyond its boundaries.

The Maryhill (Gairbraid Avenue) Housing Treatment Area in the north-west of Glasgow was officially designated in October 1970. With a population of about a thousand, Gairbraid consisted of 399 dwellings in two blocks of red sandstone tenement property. It became an arena for a community action campaign when in May 1971, at a mass meeting of residents, the Gairbraid Housing Committee (G H C) was formed to protect local interests during their rehousing by Glasgow Corporation. Throughout its campaign, the G H C touched upon almost every aspect of the rehousing process; grievances were voiced and reforms suggested, to most of which the authorities agreed. But by the end of the day, in spite of promises, very few meaningful changes had been instituted. An outline of the community's grievances provides a summary of the main features of the Corporation's rehousing policy, which will be examined here so as to explain Glasgow's reluctance to reform and to consider the implications for community action as an agency for social reform.

The problem

Cullingworth and Watson estimated[1] that in 1970 about 138,000

* Sidney Jacobs, *The Right to a Decent House*, Routledge & Kegan Paul, is forthcoming.

dwellings, 44 per cent of Glasgow's housing stock, either were without a bath or an internal w c or had serious structural defects. The official estimate[2] of houses in Glasgow failing to meet the Tolerable Standard as defined in the Housing (Scotland) Act 1969 was 75,000, roughly a quarter of the total stock. Whatever figure is accepted as the minimum, Glasgow clearly has a serious housing problem. In 1972 the city's Housing Department had a waiting list of 53,565, of whom 15,863 were classified as 'houseless families'.[3] The pressure on the Department was greatly exacerbated because much of the available accommodation is inferior both in quality and situation. As Hindess observes: 'it is certainly no longer the case that all public housing estates are considered desirable and normal places to live, even by those who can afford nothing else.'[4] All other things being equal, people usually tend to prefer a new to an old house but, if considered badly situated, a new house will not necessarily be acceptable. In 1972 Glasgow Corporation allocated 12,111 houses, of which only 3,028 were new.[5] The conditions of relets in Glasgow vary from excellent to almost entirely delapidated. Cullingworth and Watson[6] estimated that 25 per cent of public housing in Glasgow either entirely or nearly fails to meet the Tolerable Standard. The houses may also be situated anything up to seven miles from the city centre in estates which, although the size of towns, lack most of the basic amenities. In spite of poor living conditions in the old inner city, the local authority experiences difficulty in letting houses in some of these estates.[7]

The Housing Department must first solve the problem of rehousing priorities, at least to its own satisfaction, out of the mass of families in need. These must then be fitted to the houses that are available for allocation, most of which will neither be new nor generally desirable. No city can afford, financially or politically, to have a substantial number of its houses unfilled, certainly not for any length of time. The Corporation must somehow convince people to accept houses and areas which they would not choose for themselves and in which they have no desire to live. Essentially, a local authority must bully, threaten, misinform and force people into accepting houses which they do not want. Within this context, the main features of Glasgow's rehousing policy, as experienced in Gairbraid, are analysed. Only within this context, it is suggested, can this policy be fully understood.

Consultation and information

At no stage were the people of Gairbraid consulted about the demolition of their area. The decision was taken without reference to their needs, preferences or wishes. The majority had wanted to be rehoused in the vicinity but, as things turned out, the community was dispersed over a relatively wide area. The GHC felt that the decision to demolish was premature and that this directly caused many of the later difficulties. When questioned about the reasons behind their timing, the authorities simply insisted that under the Housing (Scotland) Act 1969 they were under a statutory obligation to demolish in Gairbraid. Decisions and choice were certainly involved, as Glasgow cannot simultaneously treat all the houses under its jurisdiction which fail to meet the Tolerable Standard. The GHC were never able to ascertain the reasons why their area, by no means the worst in Glasgow, was among the first to be singled out for demolition under the Act.

The principle that people have a right to be consulted about a matter as fundamental as their homes was not conceded by the Corporation. A demand for consultation is not simply an insistence on theoretical democratic rights; without proper consultation, the community is seriously disadvantaged. The GHC were forced to operate within a severely curtailed range of possibilities which had already been defined by the authorities in their own, not in the local interest. In that the people were presented with a *fait accompli*, they were not given the option of being rehoused in the new estate to be built in Gairbraid. It was also too late for them to demand that they be rehoused together, elsewhere, so that the community could be maintained. By the time they became aware of what was happening, the basic decisions about their future had long been made.

The main complaint was that (in spite of statutory obligations) insufficient account had been taken of the availability of alternative accommodation. Very few questioned the need to demolish. Professional expertise was hardly necessary for people to know that the property was inadequate and that, sooner or later, something would have to be done about it. What they were angry about was that they felt that they were being rehoused before the Corporation was properly able to do so. While by no means perfect, most houses in Gairbraid were capable of several more years of use until adequate accommodation became available. They argued that since rehousing was already being carried out in various parts of Maryhill, this ought to have been completed before a start was made in Gairbraid. In these other clearance areas, people were living in half-empty buildings, in appalling and ever deteriorating conditions. Manifestly, the Corporation was already not coping, and could certainly not deal with the additional demands generated by the Gairbraid clearance for houses in Maryhill. But this situation, of a large number of people wanting houses in a vicinity where few were available, was precisely what the local authority's action in Gairbraid precipitated.

The Corporation was able to use the existing scarcity of houses in Maryhill, although it was of their own making, to explain and justify delays in the rate of rehousing. Where the offer of a decent house to one man brings joy to him and disappointment to his neighbours, solidarity of purpose amongst the tenants may become fragile. It is obviously the kind of competitive situation that any local authority, eager to avoid organized opposition, would welcome if not deliberately create. Above all, scarcity enabled the authorities to convince people of the necessity of accepting second best. In an area where demand greatly exceeds supply, people will often try to increase their chance of an early move by opting for other less popular areas, and thus inferior houses in these relatively low amenity districts are filled. If people were fully consulted and able to participate effectively in decision-making to influence the timing of their clearance, the Corporation's difficulty in letting unwanted houses would undoubtedly increase. If rehousing in Gairbraid had been delayed until other clearances in the vicinity had been completed, and others not started until Gairbraid itself had been cleared, fewer houses outside Maryhill would have been accepted. The fact that people were not consulted, while individual choice was also limited, greatly increased the bureaucracy's power and control.

Far from being consulted, the Gairbraid residents were not even informed about the decision to demolish until the last possible moment, about a month before rehousing began. The only communication, official or otherwise, received was a Control of Occupation Order which prohibited the selling or letting of houses in the area without the local authority's prior consent. This document did not inform people about what was going to happen to the houses, and the residents, naturally enough, assumed that 'housing treatment' meant improvement, that is, that three flats would be converted into two so as to provide bathrooms. This misconception was almost universally held, apparently even by some of the local councillors. Yet, all along, the Corporation intended to demolish rather than improve the property.

The total lack of information provided in Gairbraid was not an oversight, as was later claimed.[8] The authorities never attempted to rectify the position in spite of several opportunities to do so. Requests for information—through a petition sent to the Housing Manager, through the local councillors and through various other means—were all basically ignored. The residents were kept in almost total ignorance about their future.

Since no information was provided, the GHC lodged a formal complaint against Glasgow Corporation with the Secretary of State for Scotland. In the reply received, it was stated that 'there is no statutory requirement that the making of a housing treatment area resolution should of itself be notified to the residents of the area or to the owners of the property within it.'[9] In other words, the decision to demolish a house may be taken without the occupant being told. Housing legislation seems generally to have been framed on the assumption that the local authority will act in the best interests of the residents concerned, while almost absolute power and control is vested in the local authority with few actual rights accorded to the individual.

As a result of protest by the GHC, Glasgow Corporation has undertaken to provide future treatment areas with more information. While this is a welcome reform in procedure, the information since provided falls short of what is required. In addition to knowing what is going to happen, people need to know about the timing of the treatment programme, when it is to begin and how long it will take. Most crucially, people have to know about the choice of houses likely to be made available. Such details are still not given and, while the authorities have moved some way, their provision of information is still inadequate. To tell people about the decisions taken about them is at least good public relations. Beyond that, however, a really well-informed public may not easily be persuaded to accept inferior housing, and thus very few local authorities ever supply their prospective tenants with the sort of information normally given to private home buyers.

The housing visitor's report

Glasgow's house-letting regulations state that 'departmental knowledge concerning the applicant and his family and the availability of houses will be taken into account in deciding the type and situation of the house to be offered'.[10] What is meant (but never stated) are the counter staff's impressions and the housing visitor's report. Just before the start of any rehousing, housing visitors, aptly described as 'a corps of untrained middle-aged women',[11] descend on a clearance area. Their function is to note individual preferences, to check for rent arrears, length of tenancy, eligibility for rehousing and, finally, to grade people on the basis of such criteria as 'type of people', 'cleanliness' and 'furniture'. In Gairbraid these visits lasted on average two to three minutes and some people were apparently able to be graded without even being seen. Yet the grade received largely determines the quality of the house that will be offered. It is central to house letting and, as Norman describes, 'a joint policy of grading tenants from "very good to poor" and matching them with a similarly graded house is institutionalized in the allocations system.'[12]

To be graded in this manner is to be exposed to the indignity of having to submit one's self and family to inspection and of having to allow the privacy of one's home to be invaded. The pending arrival of the housing visitor creates scenes of people hurriedly tidying and cleaning and, in some cases, even decorating. To be too proud could result in jeopardizing the chance of a decent house. Grading must create ghettos, as some estates come to be used as dumping-grounds for problem families, real or imagined. Grading conjures up a picture more in common with the objectives of the barrack-room inspection than with the provision of public housing. It can act but to demoralize.

Housing preferences are noted by the visitors, but are taken into account only when the individual is graded higher than the area of his choice or, perhaps, when both grades coincide. Tenants are usually advised to provide as wide a range of preferences as possible so as to increase their chance of satisfaction. In practice, Gairbraid residents found that where they had listed several areas they were invariably offered the least desirable, irrespective of their grading. In that preferences are noted, only an illusion of choice is created.

When confronted with the grading system used by Glasgow Corporation, a spokesman for the controlling Labour Party publicly admitted that as a means of assessment it was both 'wrong and impossible' and it was promised that, 'in future, assessment would be made on a more reasonable and factual basis'.[13] However, what resulted was simply the removal of some of the more objectionable clauses, such as 'type of people', from the classification. Thus, after considerable pressure and publicly extracted promises to reform, only negligible changes were made in the grading system. Altering the form's wording, if anything, will serve only to disguise its purpose, making future protest more difficult. In so far as grading and allocation is concerned, the prospective council house tenant in Glasgow is now still judged in exactly the same unfair and arbitrary way as were the people of Gairbraid. In other words, the principles involved in the grading system have survived the Gairbraid campaign to emerge basically unscathed.

As a means of accurate assessment, the grading system can have little value. It is without any semblance of scientific validity or reliability, and thus as a means of classification it is essentially nonsense. However, to attack its validity may miss the point, for it may not be meant to function as an accurate measure at all. Whatever else it fails to do, the grading system gives the Housing Department authority and power and provides it with an instrument of control. A tenant cannot be told that he is being offered a house because of a draw out of a hat. Allocations need authority and the aura of expertise that surrounds a formal system. The requirement is not accuracy or even fairness—which, under the circumstances, are near impossible to achieve—but rather, to increase the possibility of acquiescence. Above all else, the Housing Department needs docility and acceptance of its decisions, and its decisions need at least to appear reasonably consistent and impartial. The grading system performs these functions. It provides an inherently chaotic situation with a rationale, order and a feeling of finality—if one offer matches personal grading, so will the next, and therefore to refuse the first may seem pointless.

In the above terms, the grading system is not a lunatic measure that, in the face of all contrary evidence, for some inexplicable bureaucratic reason, the Corporation insists on retaining. On the contrary, it is seen to be the very essence of housing policy. In addition to being both relatively easy and inexpensive to administer—no specially trained staff are required—it ensures that the Corporation firmly controls all house allocation decisions. It fills unwanted houses. The feeble and meaningless changes to the visitor's form can thus be understood. Short of the Housing Department grinding to a halt, there was never any real possibility of the changes being otherwise. So, too, the reluctance to grant the principle of rehousing communities *en bloc* may be explained.[14] To do so on any large scale would involve scrapping the grading system.

Communication

The individual wishing to enquire, inform, request or complain has to take his case to the Housing Department. There he must wait sometimes several hours before his name is called and he is seen, usually by an over-worked junior clerk who will have neither the time nor the authority to be of much assistance. Invariably, Gairbraid residents were rudely treated, given misinformation and false promises and were frequently threatened with eviction and 'no more offers' when houses in absolutely disgraceful condition were refused.

Faced with criticism, the Department's solution was to replace the staff concerned with others of a 'more mature age', although the Housing Manager made it clear that he was doing so under duress.[15] Thus, while some improvement in the quality of service was obtained, no fundamental change had occurred: there was no guarantee that the new counter clerks would never emulate their younger colleagues. The replacement of personnel may provide scapegoats but does not necessarily alter very much else. It certainly does not admit to any faults in the system. Although no longer generally subjected to extremely abusive behaviour, the residents' basic difficulty of gaining access to authority still remained.

Accordingly, the GHC proposed to give a senior official responsibility for each clearance area in the city and assign special times when he would be available for interview. This proposal was designed to create an avenue of communication between officials and residents so that the former could be freely accessible. In this way, account could have been taken of changing family circumstances where special attention might be paid to rent arrears, the elderly, the medically unfit, the timid, and others otherwise neglected by the system. Further, it would have created the opportunity for officialdom to explain their difficulties and thus allow for a compromise to be reached between availability of houses in particular areas and individual preferences.

At a specially convened meeting which included the Housing Convenor, his deputy and senior officials, the authorities agreed that the GHC delegation's proposals were practical and sensible and that they would definitely be instituted. It seemed that, at long last, the GHC had achieved a meaningful reform. However, without explanation and without even bothering to inform the GHC, the

Corporation, on the advice of the Housing Manager, changed its mind.

The proposals, by making the authorities more accessible and the officials accountable, would certainly have curtailed much of the bureaucracy's power. For the tenant, it would have increased the supply of reliable information and, to a degree, would have dispelled uncertainty and feelings of helplessness. Face-to-face interviews with senior staff, to be demanded as of right, could help hasten the rehousing process, facilitate choice and participation in decision-making. In other words, some transfer of power was involved and, as such, the G H C proposals were not merely administrative reforms but threatened fundamental policy objectives. It is suggested that, once these implications had been appreciated and real participation seen as a possible consequence of its implementation, the reform was immediately doomed.

A policy of divide and rule

In summary, Glasgow's rehousing policy and practice, as applied in Gairbraid, was characterized, through every stage, by a maximum of bureaucratic control and a minimum of citizen participation. It was designed neither to consult nor inform and excluded those affected from all decision-making. In its implementation it created anxiety, distress and, above all, uncertainty. It severely limited choice and the individual was accorded few rights. It dealt with the community, in colonial fashion, by divide and rule, isolating the individual through scarcity and competition. Power was concentrated within the bureaucracy, and exercised so that little was predictable and much arbitrary. In short, it was essentially undemocratic.

The absence of democracy from Glasgow's rehousing policy is by no means unique, as most of our cities seem to operate a more or less similar system. Why do the British working class tolerate it? Because the organized labour movement has not concerned itself with community, as distinct from industrial, problems, the individual caught up in the rehousing process has been largely left to his own devices and has therefore had very little choice but to accept the existing administrative procedures. He can, although not without difficulty, make his needs and preferences known, but if he is dissatisfied, there is very little he can do. The exception is when urgent possession is required of his property, in which case he can refuse to move unless satisfactorily accommodated. Here, too,

however, the authorities have a flexibility of action denied th
tenant. He 'sits-out' at his own peril. He must correctly ascertain th
degree of urgency with which his property is wanted, and suc
information is not always easily obtainable. If wrong, he will simpl
be ignored and left in conditions which increasingly becom
intolerable. If, however, they do want him out quickly, he then face
the threat and possibility of eviction which, in the last resort, th
authorities have at their command. Whatever action the tenan
takes, it is without the assurance that it will be worth it, that he wi
ultimately succeed. He can but wage a war of nerves. In a battl
between the individual and the institution, it will most certainly b
the former who expends the nervous energy, for it is he and not th
institution who stands to gain or lose.

The individual awaits the offer of accommodation with n
certainty of when or where this will be. If he rejects an offer, he doe
not know when the next will arrive or whether it will be a
improvement. Glasgow's house-letting regulations are hardly
charter of tenant rights: 'If an applicant refuses any offer for reason
which in the opinion of the Housing Manager are not good an
sufficient, consideration of the application may be suspended for
period of up to one year.'[16] The above clause exemplifies th
discretionary power of the local authority, determining who wi
receive what house, where, and deciding for the individual what i
'good and sufficient'. Such decisions are without obligation t
justify or explain and are unhindered by rights of appeal. It amount
to almost absolute control of the supply and allocation of house
and establishes a relationship between local authority and tenan
which is one of superiority-inferiority, of power and dependence

The system is unjust and is seen to be unjust. It is tolerated, a
least partially, because it has the power to reward. The individua
enters the rehousing process in the hope that he will be among thos
favoured. He is not likely to complain about the lack of
participatory democracy if he is offered the house of his choice.
Housing Departments are able to function successfully because they
deal with individuals and not communities. No matter how
capricious a system, those whom it rewards will not tend to
challenge or question it and thus, for organized opposition,
solidarity of purpose is difficult to achieve and easily broken. As
long as it is a decent house that is wanted, and it is unreasonable to
expect initial opposition to rehousing policy on any other basis, the
advantage remains with the local authority. Simply, a suitable offer

annot be refused merely because a neighbour has not been given the
ame. Protest based on individual aspirations, and not on principle or
deology, is obviously vulnerable.

Glasgow, in common with other local authorities, rehouses its
enants one by one over a lengthy period of time.[17] Through
ontinual rehousing, an organized local group will increasingly be
veakened by depopulation, with loss to its leadership and support.
nevitably, numbers will decline to a point after which opposition
vill no longer be viable, and then defeat will have to be admitted.
he G H C was able to extend its activities because members agreed to
emain active after being rehoused, which postponed but did not
void final impotence. When only twenty families, about 5 per cent
f the original population, remained in the area, the committee lost
ts power of protest and these families had basically to fend for
hemselves.

Housing policy is designed to divide and rule, to deal with
ndividuals rather than communities. The advantages of maintaining
xisting communities are obvious and are acknowledged by most
ocal authorities, including Glasgow. Nevertheless, rehousing
ommunities *en bloc* is rarely attempted, perhaps because this
nvolves a real transfer of power to the local community. While an
ndividual may be forced to accept an unwanted relet, a community
s less likely to be as easily coerced. The local authority often dare
ot, by creating a single community interest, dispel the belief that
every man is for himself'.

Rehousing through fear of flood and fire

To function properly, an authoritarian system requires acqui-
scence. It cannot easily accommodate criticism—insistence on even
he most elementary of rights is usually perceived as 'trouble-
naking'. To achieve docility, the system must have the ability to
enalize malcontents. A housing department has this power in that it
an withhold offers: control over the flow of allocations gives it its
orce of sanction. In deciding whether to accept or reject an offer,
he individual faces the implicit and often loudly articulated threat
hat to refuse may mean being left until last before being rehoused.
To refuse an offer may incur a sentence of years in limbo, of being
eft to stagnate.

To be among the last to be rehoused from a clearance area means months and even years of living under intolerable and often dangerous conditions, especially in tenements where even one empty flat may signify ruin for the whole building. It is a life of coping with one crisis after another, of living with rising damp and dry rot, of learning to manage without running water, functioning toilets or electricity, of never being able to leave the house unattended. Clearance areas invariably become centres of attraction for vandalism and petty theft. Houses are frequently flooded, ceilings collapse and backcourts become cesspools strewn with much and rubbish, where mice and rats abound. In all this, the individual can do little except endure and hope that tomorrow's post will bring an offer from the Corporation. In short, to be left in a clearance area is sheer hell. Worst of all is the fear of fire, in or around the affected area.

During one five-day period, the fire brigade was called to Gairbraid eighteen times (which does not count the fires put out by the residents themselves). If the Gairbraid experience is at all typical and there is no reason to believe otherwise, then Glasgow's Housing Department bears responsibility, at least indirectly, for a significant number of the fires in the city.[18] Children started fires in Gairbraid sometimes with near-tragic consequences, merely so that fire engines could be seen in action. Though the problem of vandalism is seldom considered within the context of housing policy, prolonged rehousing is certainly a contributory factor, providing as it does ideal training grounds and lengthy apprenticeships for young vandals.

It hardly needs to be demonstrated that, under such conditions, people may accept houses they would otherwise have rejected. However, this limitation on the freedom of choice restricts not only those last in the area but the first out, for the fear of being left tarnishes the whole process from beginning to end. Rehousing has been going on in Glasgow long enough for everyone to know at least something of what is involved. It is a part of working-class Glasgow culture. Housing conditions need to be pretty horrific to make news in Glasgow and yet, every now and then, the plight of a family in some appalling predicament is highlighted by the local press and television. Most people have relatives and friends who have previously been through the rehousing process. Indeed, much of the city still looks as if it has just emerged from an aerial bombardment and at night, almost everywhere, lights can be seen shining from a window in what is otherwise a deserted ruin, telling of a family still awaiting rehousing long after the bulk of the population has been moved. Everyone's bus-route passes these sights. Just down the Maryhill Road from Gairbraid, partly-occupied derelict buildings existed before and during the entire life of the treatment area. Gairbraid was fed on the horrors of previous clearance areas, and those left there until last will in turn contribute their own particular chapter to the ever-continuing saga that is Glasgow's rehousing policy. When clearance comes to any area, most people there will know what to expect.

It is not necessary to argue that delays in rehousing are deliberately engineered so as to create fear. It is sufficient merely to point to the fact that rehousing in Glasgow takes on average two years to complete, near the end of which time conditions are quite intolerable. Even if it is not the official intention to create such a situation, it does arise as a consequence of policy of which the authorities are fully aware, while they do nothing to ameliorate the situation for those in the area. The fear of being left until last before being rehoused, which in Gairbraid was probably deliberately reinforced by the staff, was an important factor influencing the acceptance of offers long before conditions had actually deteriorated. For this fear to have a potency, it is not necessary for the area to have already declined, but for the tenants merely to be sure that sooner or later it will. In these terms, the prolonged clearance of an area leading to intolerable living conditions is not an unfortunate but unavoidable aftermath of policy. On the contrary, it is what enables policy to work.

To shorten the time between when the first and last tenant leaves would certainly involve administrative difficulties. For example, co-ordination, planning and greater efficiency would be required, which in themselves may go some way in explaining the local authority's reluctance to hasten the process. Yet changes do not seem beyond the realm of human endeavour. Much misery could be avoided, such as by rehousing people close by close instead of randomly selecting them from all over the area. Rehousing could be carefully co-ordinated with specific building programmes. As an area runs down, effective temporary repairs and maintenance, certainly of the essential services, could be carried out with greater diligence, and proper police protection provided. Indeed, there is room for considerable improvement in all spheres of the rehousing process. The effort and expense involved seem little price to pay when compared with what exists; particularly in Scotland where the predominance of tenement property ensures that the consequences of prolonged rehousing will be drastic. However, to do so would remove the 'big stick' from housing policy. Remove the element of fear, and control is weakened. It would deprive the administration of its teeth, as the force of sanction is vital to the implementation of present policy: it is fear that cements the process, creating acquiescence. As long as rehousing policy exists in its present form, the result—people suffering in intolerable conditions—will remain and cannot be changed without radically altering the whole process.

Implications

During its campaign, the G H C generated considerable publicity which adversely reflected on Glasgow's rehousing policy and practice. In response, the authorities acknowledged deficiencies in most aspects of the rehousing process and, although reforms were promised, only marginal changes were ever achieved. This reluctance to reform is explained, on the one hand, by Glasgow's enormous demand for decent houses and, on the other, by an acute housing shortage, severely exacerbated by the inferior quality and situation of many of those which are available. In other words, Glasgow faces an almost impossible task. Under prevailing circumstances, it is suggested that, for the Housing Department to function, if the present policy did not exist, it would have had to have been invented. It is undemocratic because it must be.

In the discussion of various aspects of Glasgow's rehousing policy and practice, it has been argued that the authorities appear to have very little room in which to manoeuvre and, basically, only marginal reform seems possible. This is not to say that there cannot be concessions to individuals or even groups of people, particularly if they manage to shout loudly. Indeed, Gairbraid achieved a great many concessions. However, these are always regarded as special cases in need of preferential treatment; in other words, exceptions to the rules which do not alter basic policy. Thus, they do not alter our assumption that, as the system now stands, reform is not possible.

Different aspects of policy taken singly may appear to be irrational and even self-defeating but, seen together, as mutually supportive parts of an integral system, each becomes comprehensible. This argues strongly against the feasibility of attempting piecemeal reform. On these grounds, the relatively few changes achieved by the G H C may be understood. In Gairbraid, local priorities were continually forced to change as different aspects of policy were applied in the area. Thus, pressure could not be maintained on any one grievance long enough to ensure that promised reforms were instituted. For example, when it became clear that the housing visitor's form had not been significantly altered, the residents had long since been graded and were by then, quite rightly, interested in other more immediately relevant issues. Thus, community action in Gairbraid was forced by the demands of the situation to seek piecemeal reform where only total change was possible.

What of the future? Various pundits[19] predict the imminent solution of Glasgow's housing shortage. As a concomitant, it could be argued that as demand for houses decreases, so will policy become liberalized. However, the easing of demand is unlikely in itself to produce reform. Meaningful local participation will more probably be achieved through pressure from the grass roots than from policy decisions at the top. Moreover, given present national and local government priorities, neither in Glasgow nor anywhere else in urban Britain is the housing shortage likely to be overcome in the foreseeable future. Community action needs to concentrate on what exists rather than on what some administrators or academics think might happen. From the bleak standpoint of present-day reality in Glasgow, visions of a future where no new public housing needs to be built seem foolishly premature and quite utopian. Certainly, in clearance areas, community action has a role to perform, although its precise nature may not be altogether clear.

Community action, with limited resources and geographically localized within a relatively small area, cannot be expected to dent the prevailing power structure. It simply attempts to 'chip away' at existing inequalities in the hope that the accumulative effect may eventually lead to some real reforms. It is a strategy of change through nuisance value which, if persistently applied, may produce some positive results, but only where the system is able easily to accommodate change. Housing reform is extremely unlikely to be achieved in this manner. If community action is to pursue social reform in housing, it will need to mobilize a great deal more power than hitherto.

This is not to deprecate the achievements of community action in organizing small areas around single issues—merely to say that the implications of such successes are necessarily limited. What was required in Gairbraid, if bureaucratic control was to be seriously threatened, was to organize and ally in co-ordinated action several clearance areas spread throughout the city. If rehousing policy cannot be reformed, it needs to be totally changed; but real change will take place only through the power of mass organization able to force a radical overhaul. It may be that a head-on collision is necessary whereby the local authority is forced to admit that it cannot cope and that it will no longer continue to function as the vehicle through which impossible central government policies are administered. A massive infusion of capital is required: as Michael Barratt Brown points out,[20] the £1,000 million that successive governments have spent on the development of Concorde could have built 250,000 houses. Community action needs to ensure not only that a great many more houses are built but also that a meaningful measure of local control is exercised over the rehousing process.

Community action, however, as presently financed—sponsored by either local authorities, charitable trusts or the universities—is unable to provide the resources necessary to mount a challenge on the scale required. As Bryant notes,[21] support may need to be gained from the trade unions if community action is to win the 'big issues'. To do so, community action must first accept its inherently political function and abandon its pretensions of being a non ideological third alternative to the established political order or to the sectarian Left. Community action, if it is meaningfully to contribute to social reform, must attempt to forge for itself a place, independent if possible, within the mainstream of working-class politics.

Notes

1 J. B. Cullingworth and C. J. Watson, *Housing in Clydeside 1970*, HMSO, Edinburgh, 1971, p. 58.
2 Corporation of the City of Glasgow and Scottish Development Department, *Report of the Glasgow Housing Programme Working Party 1970*, p. 8.
3 Housing Management Department, Corporation of the City of Glasgow, *Annual Report 1972*, p. 15.
4 Barry Hindess, *The Decline of Working-Class Politics*, Paladin, 1971, p. 53.
5 *Annual Report 1972*, p. 13.
6 Op.cit., p. 60.
7 R. D. Mansley, *Areas of Need in Glasgow*, Corporation of Glasgow, 1972, p. 10. Mansley, Glasgow's Director of Planning, draws attention to the number of relets which the Housing Manager has difficulty in letting. He wrongly interprets this as indicating a decrease in demand, omitting to consider the inferior quality, in terms of type, condition, age and situation, of the houses difficult to let.

8 The Corporation attempted to excuse the lack of information provided in Gairbraid by the fact that the area was among the first to be dealt with under the 1969 Act and, therefore, claimed that the proper procedures had not yet been formulated. However, it may be argued that as local people are even less familiar with housing legislation than are the authorities, greater rather than less diligence in the application of new legislation is required to ensure that people are kept fully informed.

9 Letter to the Gairbraid Housing Committee from the Scottish Development Department, 16 December 1971.

10 House Letting Regulations, quoted in *Annual Report 1972*, p. 56.

11 *Glasgow News*, no. 5, 6–19 December 1971.

12 Peter Norman, 'A derelict policy', *Official Architecture and Planning*, January 1972, p. 32.

13 Quoted from BBC Scotland, 'Current Account', televised on 15 October 1971.

14 Malcolm Smith, Glasgow's Housing Manager, was a member of a Joint Working Party on Community Problems, set up on 8 December 1967, which considered that 'an artificial community' was at least partially created by established communities not being rehoused together. Glasgow has since not adopted a policy of rehousing communities or even close relatives together.

15 *Glasgow Herald*, 18 April 1972. Also *Annual Report 1971*, p. 7. In this, the Housing Manager stated that although staff had been replaced, 'a substantial part of the criticism was unwarranted'.

16 House Letting Regulations, p. 57.

17 In Glasgow's favour, it should be noted that, unlike some local authorities, the city's Housing Department does not tend to shunt families from one clearance area to another. On the whole, people are not moved into property which has a limited life.

18 After the fire at St George's Cross on 18 November 1972 in which two people died and thirty-one were injured, Mrs Ballantyne, convenor of Glasgow's police and fire committee, suggested that steps be taken to have all derelict property demolished and that special precautions were needed where shops stood empty beneath occupied tenements: *Glasgow Herald*, 20 November 1972.

19 Mansley, op.cit.; Norman, op.cit.

20 Michael Barratt Brown, 'The worker's pound', *Bulletin of the Institute of Workers' Control*, no. 10, 1973, p. 36.

21 Richard Bryant, 'Community action', *British Journal of Social Work*, 2 (2), 1972, p. 214

Part II Training and the Development of Community Work as a Profession

The de-professionalisation of community work

D.J. Cox and N.J. Derricourt

t the annual general meeting in June 1973, the five year-
ld Association of Community Workers in effect opened up
nembership to anyone who could define him- or herself as a
ommunity worker. Previously, membership had been restricted to
nose who had a specified educational qualification and at least two
ears' appropriate experience, or no qualification and three years'
xperience.[1] Until then only teachers of community work courses
ecognised by the A C W had been (from September 1971) offered
ull membership without such qualifications or experience. A
nembership sub-committee had determined the appropriateness of
xperience. The change to an open door policy would appear to be a
najor turning point for the A C W and may indicate some important
hanges in the development of community work in Britain. It is also
nteresting sociologically as an example of an occupation which has
oluntarily turned back from what is widely regarded as a key step in
ne 'professionalisation process' and as an essential trait of any 'fully
ledged profession'.[2]

In this article we intend to explore the present situation of
ommunity work as an occupation, and the occupational strategies
vailable to representative bodies like the A C W. The dilemmas facing
ommunity work and those who aspire to be paid a 'living wage' for
oing it will be examined in terms of (i) the inherent characteristics
f the work and (ii) the socio-cultural context in which it is
eveloping. We think that our analysis provides a rationale for the
ew policies that appear to be emerging in the A C W.

Community work and professionalism

Gerald Popplestone made an ambitious first attempt[3] to analyse the
ormation of the A C W in the context of sociological approaches to

professionalisation and occupational ideology. His thesis was tha the A C W consisted of a jumble of practitioners in various fields an activities (Councils of Social Service, Youth and Communit Service, Community Social Work and numerous *ad hoc* jobs with 'community' flavour) who had no coherent ideology or body o knowledge but who shared a concern for establishing statu legitimacy and career structures for themselves. Popplestone saw th A C W as a vehicle whereby these groups under the broad lab 'community work' could acquire professional status and a occupational identity, and he feared that people who saw themselve as community workers were bent on an occupational strategy whic would vitiate community work's theoretically 'client-centrec viewpoint. He then showed how the activities of these group conformed to his predetermined model of the development of profession, a model which appears to be largely derived from th work of Wilensky[4] and Bucher and Strauss.[5] Popplestone's critique useful and makes a number of interesting points about the way i which community participation has caught on as a panacea i government and local government circles,[6] the different interes groups and ideologies involved, the tendency to blur thes differences in the term 'community work', and the conflictin loyalties to agency and fellow-workers or to 'client' groups tha beset community workers.

Popplestone concluded from a 1970 A C W membership list tha 61 per cent of the members worked for Councils of Social Service o held administrative posts in voluntary or statutory organisations while 12 per cent were 'grass-roots' workers. Our analysis of th most recent membership list shows that 30 per cent of members i July 1973 were people whose designation would lead us to suppos that they spent most of their time working in the field at grass-roots level (although few were actually employed b grass-roots groups). Of these just under half had joined betwee November 1972 and July 1973. The number of members whose job are mostly administrative (40 per cent) still exceeds the number o grass-roots workers—but the proportion has clearly changed Members in academic or training jobs and students account for 2 per cent—both have increased rapidly in the last year. One could sa that the administrative workers have lost the overall majorit attributed to them by Popplestone. A significant 'greening' o membership has occurred.[7]

The problem is that the recent move to open up A C W membershi not predictable from Popplestone's analysis. This indicated a strong pressure to greater professionalisation in terms of restriction of entry and increased separation from the needs and aspirations of the client. Although he illuminated a number of obstacles in the way of 'full' professional status there is no doubt that, for him, both internal and external pressures were pushing in that direction. He underestimated at least three things: the wish of an apparently significant number of people to maintain a 'client-centred' viewpoint; the extent to which the dilemmas were already being discussed; and the ACW's determination not be left in the rearguard of community work thought.

The ACW appears now to be a body acting in a way uncharacteristic of the aspiring professional organisation anxious to accumulate enough scores to make the grade. If we still talk in terms of a unilinear model, then the recent conference decision was a step back on the continuum which leads from a mere occupation to an honoured profession. To understand the present situation of the ACW requires first the abandonment of the conceptual model of the 'emerging profession' that constrains Popplestone's analysis and, second, a full study of the complex empirical changes in the composition and strengths of the interest groups with a finger in the community work pie. Unfortunately, we have not the space to undertake the latter in full, but we do hope to show how the ACW itself was moved to take this decision.

The ACW policy change

The Manchester 1973 AGM decision showed that a large part of the membership clearly believed that an exclusive membership/admissions policy clashed with one of the main purposes of community work. In fact, to distinguish between a person who had a Community Work or Social Administration Diploma and a full-time community work job, and another person who had left school at sixteen and had had long experience as secretary of a tenants' association seemed to raise contradictions which full-time paid community workers either could not accept or could not rationalise effectively. Moreover, it seemed to be becoming less likely that one would ever be able to define community work as a discrete body of knowledge whose outward signs distinguish community workers from other people. For example, the occupations of planning and adult education were already well represented on the ACW Council itself, and it was obvious that here were members who identified themselves with another occupation, even profession, and yet regarded some community work skills and knowledge as an important aid to their work. To some, the Manchester decision was *hara-kiri*, to others naiveté, and to still others the only honest thing to do. However surprising the strength of feeling may have been on the day, the decision itself was not unexpected.

Both at meetings of the initial steering group and at meetings held to discuss the formation of the ACW, the choice between an open association and an exclusive one was discussed openly. Though no one was for a very exclusive association, very few advocated a completely open one either, although it was suggested. Most people became involved in an argument over the choice between a membership policy determined by training and experience, and a more open association. From 1970 onwards the tension between the needs and realities of grass-roots community work and the promotion of a credible professional body was often discussed in association meetings,[8] although usually in the context of discussion about two other issues: the relationship between social work and community work (hence that between the British Association of Social Workers and the ACW), and the difficulty of judging the appropriateness of educational qualifications and experience. It was not until early 1972 that the argument over the choice between an open association or an exclusive one really came to a head again.

The most important reason why the initial steering group had decided in 1968 to suggest an exclusive association was that, at the time, it was hoped that the ACW could become part of the emerging BASW, for which some degree of exclusiveness was understood to be necessary. In the event, by the end of 1969, the ACW knew that it would not be acceptable to BASW, but by then the ACW had been inaugurated and the constitution settled for the time being. One would judge that the initiators of the ACW had thought that community work, or at least a significant kind of community work, would best be promoted by attaching it to social work. It is likely that both the character of the initial group and the then current state of community work consciousness reinforced that view. Whatever the reasons, the apparent goal of professionalism probably alienated many people who, at field level, could not escape the paradoxes. The 'closed shop' was to a certain extent mediated by the provisions of an associate membership category for anyone who did not have the stipulated experience or educational qualifications. But there were clearly some very competent, not to say illustrious, community workers who were not eligible for full membership under the original rules and who were not mollified by the associate category.

A sharp increase in membership following the alteration of admission rules might not only merely indicate that more people were eligible, but could support the view that some potential members had previously been alienated. Whatever happens, it is already clear from our analysis of the membership that the number of people likely to identify with a 'grass-roots' interest has increased proportionate numerical decrease in some of the other interests, e.g. Councils of Social Service administrators.[9] It is interesting that e.g. Councils of Social Service administrators.[9] It is interesting that the training lobby has grown, and that the number of statutory administrators in membership now exceeds the number of their voluntary counterparts. We conclude that an alliance of 'grass-roots oriented' members from all occupational categories (whether administration or field or a mixture of both) will generally dictate the direction and interests of A C W policy for the foreseeable future.

Professionalism reconsidered

Terence Johnson suggests[10] that the 'Sociology of the Professions' has been too ready to adopt the professions' own definitions of themselves as its analytic categories. In doing so, he claims, they have tended to accept an institutionalised form of control over occupations, peculiar to the specific historical conditions of nineteenth-century Anglo-American culture, as the essential condition of 'professional' occupations. This is equally true of functionalist approaches which stress the integrative role professions play in society, and feature common ideology and body of knowledge as essential characteristics of professional communities,[11] and of 'trait' approaches which identify a number of features common to all professions[12] or identify the essential stages of professionalisation. Derivative discussions on the professional ambitions of a very wide range of occupations tend to assess their chances of acquiring the features of a 'true' profession and speculate on whether the lack of certain key attributes (such as an independent body of knowledge) condemns some unfortunate occupations to the limbo state of semi-professions.[13] Some aspiring occupational spokesmen try to get the concept redefined in some way so that the legitimacy, status, autonomy and 'success' associated with the medical and legal professions can be assumed by their own occupational group.[14] Adopting the rhetoric of professionalism as part of an opportunist occupational strategy i almost universal among the plethora of white-collar trades that wish to avoid the stigma of trade unionism. It is not just social workers—bingo callers now have a code of ethics, driving instructors have successfully differentiated themselves from amateurs, etc.

Many critics of the professional aspirations of groups such as social workers and community workers are constrained by the same analytic model described by Johnson. The 'helping professions' are castigated for restricting entry, developing esoteric jargon, raising qualifications and generally status-seeking in the middle-class hierarchy.[15] It is claimed that professionalisation necessarily consists of acquiring the characteristics of the old professions and with them the tendency to conservatism, mystification and an increasing separation from the needs and aspirations of clients. For community workers and social workers, gaining professional status is seen by their radical critics as being accompanied by a rejection of radical strategies of social change and a willingness to be used as agents of social control.

An alternative way of looking at occupational organisation emerges from Johnson's book. He suggests that 'Collegiate Professionalism' is but one form of institutionalised control over an occupation. In this form the producer–consumer relationship is controlled by the producers; they define the client's needs and determine how they are to be satisfied. This powerful position is supported by legislation and gives the occupation a very high degree of control over its own and its consumers' affairs. Establishing this form of control, typified by medicine and the law, was possible only at a particular time in a particular culture, because practitioners with a monopoly of widely-needed skills and high social position were much more powerful than a dispersed and unorganised mass of consumers. Other forms of institutionalised control are patronage, where the consumer defines his own needs and judges how well the producer satisfies them. The patron can be a wealthy individual (oligarchic patronage) as with nineteenth-century architects, or a large bureaucratic organisation (corporate patronage) as with most accountants, surveyors, personnel officers or librarians. Thus members of many so-called professions are in a very different tuation, as staff employees, from the traditional professions njoying full collegiate control. Last, Johnson talks about nediation', where a third party (e.g. the state) mediates between roducer and consumer, defining needs and judging satisfaction. ocial work is, perhaps, the clearest example of state mediation; the :ate guarantees the consumers, sets up the welfare organisations and irgely controls entry and standards for the occupation.

For all the ideology and rhetoric of professionalism, it seems that ew emerging occupations need not, and in most cases cannot,)llow any predetermined path laid down by the established rofessions. There is really no chance of community work becoming new and powerful profession, as Popplestone and some of the)unders of A C W seemed to assume it could.

The inadequacy of the professionalisation model is illustrated by)me research on American social workers by Epstein.[16] In his imple of 899 full-time social workers in New York he found that iere was not an integrated professional community—that is, social orkers did not see themselves as primarily loyal to a 'profession'. urthermore, the more 'professional' the social workers were in :rms of qualifications, the more radical they were. 'This evidence iggests that the effect of staffing a social work agency with more ighly professional workers (using education as the criteria) is to reate a more change-oriented, conflicting-tolerating milieu'.[17] pstein's research appears to conflict with the predictions of opplestone or Cannan,[18] and suggests that conventional categories f profession, professionalisation, professional role orientation, etc. re not really explaining what is going on even in occupations like)cial work which is often assumed to be far along the road to rofessional status. In community work, the situation is likely to be ven more complex, and both the advocates and the critics of rofessionalisation are using outdated categories which may obscure ie real possibilities and alternatives open to occupational ssociations such as the A C W. Perhaps community work is not stuck n the horns of a dilemma: either to professionalise and end up as an soteric, exclusive, 'neutral' bunch of Ph.D. 'change agents', or to ass into oblivion with no place on pay scales, no training courses, nd their 'thing' carved up by the more 'successful' professions irking on the side-lines.

Who wants community work?

It was probably unpredictable that there would be such an increas[e] in the demand, particularly among the young, but also among tho[se] with pedigrees of CND vintage, for 'radical work', or what migh[t] perhaps be termed 'conscientious work'. There is clearly a growin[g] demand by students and would-be community workers; in fac[t] community work seems to be becoming the inevitable destination [of] many different kinds of activists. This is in part caused by the fa[ct] that many other (perhaps more desirable) avenues are closed t[o] them—labour unions are an example of this. One would guess th[at] the links with the radical student establishment will grow, but if o[ne] were to look at Young Volunteer Force, Student Communit[y] Action and such organisations as Task Force now, one cou[ld] probably discern a good deal of interlocking interest, although o[f] nothing like the scale that has been seen in America. Thu[s] placements can be a useful input in more ways than one; they n[ot] only can provide valuable resources for field agencies, but als[o] generate a commitment to the work on the part of students. F[or] some students, where the placement is of a satisfactory length, it ca[n] be like a first job. The demand for training brings with it a certa[in] amount of pedagogic paraphernalia—trainers, books, conference[s] seminars, validated courses and general academic pomp an[d] circumstance.

Epstein's research would suggest that, for American soci[al] workers, longer training has a radicalising influence, and the high[ly] qualified may not aspire to traditional professional status. Length[y] exposure to education and the contemporary student milieu may b[e] expected to have a different effect from, for example, medical [or] legal socialisation. It could be that the future of community wor[k] depends on an alliance between these two groups of dissimil[ar] origin—the highly trained refugees from the middle class, and the heroes, the self-taught community leaders.

The keen interest of would-be community workers contras[ts] remarkably with the lack of demand from would-be consum[er] localities; this cannot all be explained by the newness of communit[y] work and the localities' ignorance of what community work has t[o] offer, nor do we think that community work has in gener[al] embraced a pathological interpretation of locality problems whic[h] would be unacceptable to local people. The simple fact is th[at] localities are generally suspicious, as they have had reasons for bein[g] that community work may be used as a control strategy by local government and others who have the means of influence. This will not be changed unless enough community work is done that is generally seen to be beneficial and trustworthy. There are other complications which probably affect a 'client view' of community workers, including the possible risk of labelling and other risks attached to being involved in something unfamiliar which may fail. Moreover, although community workers usually use language which is more easily understood than that of local government officers, people find it bizarre that someone should seem to want to build a faith out of mundane words and actions.

It is clear that several other fields of work are interested in either using some of community work, or of absorbing some of it. This is true to varying extents of planning, adult education, social work, youth work and the churches. This cuts two ways: on the one hand, the wooed object shines with a finer light; on the other, it could do much to undermine the idea of community work as an important activity with significant values in any sense, and to relegate it to the kind of instrumental role which administration enjoys. There are pressures to legitimise forms of community work from the Home Office (through CDP and the Urban Programme), the DoE and the DES, quite apart from the sponsorship of voluntary organisations by local authorities. While decisions to sponsor community work may be made in times of quandary (and perhaps regretted later), a major underlying concern of government intervention must be to regulate the forms of community work practised legitimately and to regulate the scope of actual projects, so that its intervention is seen to be effectual but not dangerous. Employing well-known radicals is one way of attesting seriousness. Local authorities have been a bit more careful, but the number of community work posts advertised by local authority departments has increased enormously.[19]

Community work has avoided being confined within one profession, whether old or new, and has also avoided being confined to 'paid work'. Not only is it now well known that paid and unpaid people may be doing similar things, but the recent growth of interest in Britain in 'new careers' and training for 'indigenous non-professionals' has emphasised that 'local people' may with some help do many jobs as well or better than middle-class outsiders. Work which full-time paid community workers do in their 'paid time' becomes indistinguishable from what others do unpaid. This is bound to lead to a spread of interest in community work, although it makes life less simple for full-time workers.

Finally, there is considerable argument about the actual benefit of community work to its 'client populations'. John Benington ha clearly made the point[20] that there is no guarantee that information gathered by community workers is used primarily to benefit the deprived; perhaps one of the main contributions of CDP will be to explore and document the mechanics of community work's usefulness. In the meantime, even while some workers may become highly adept at exploiting 'the ambiguities of the situation', the uncertainty of potential benefits is bound to worry both community workers and supposed beneficiaries; it really means that we cannot generalise about the relative benefits of community work to client and corporation. It is clear that there is a considerable two-fold demand—for community work, and for definition, although the different sources of demand are looking for different definitions.

Strategies for community workers

Turning away from a strategy of imitative professionalisation appears to be an entirely realistic course of action for the ACW. A state-supported collegiate control of community work after the model of the traditional professions is laughable as an objective. Community work skills are not particularly well defined; they are as much derived from experience as training, while many of them are supposed to be readily developed among the clients themselves. Mystifying these skills must go against many of the tenets of community work as an activity. More important, since community work is unlikely to become a major occupation for the second or even the third sons of the gentry, it does not enjoy the political pull that established medicine and the law in the nineteenth century. Powerful government and local government bureaucracies are among the major employers of full-time community workers, and such powerful consumers are unlikely for long to give them any more scope and autonomy than their other expert employees. This is especially so as community work must in some ways be a threat to the establishment, hence all the more need to maintain 'quality control'. If professional control is impossible, then following the professional rhetoric and disguised trade union strategy of the BASW is unlikely to be a more successful tactic for the ACW. The BASW's strength lies in the fact that the vast majority of social workers are employed in similar work situations by large local government departments (state mediation in Johnson's terms). This provides a reasonably centralised decision-making process whereby the B A S W can negotiate over working conditions, career structures, training, etc. as a representative body. The B A S W does not really control the profession; it is far weaker than the employers. It can, however, represent social workers' special interests with more respectability than N A L G O. The other employers in voluntary social work tend to lag slightly behind local government in pay and conditions, offering (usually) more autonomy in return.

In community work there is a much wider diversity of employers and work situations, and there is no large employer to be used to set standards. The structural basis for a successful trade union strategy is just not there at the moment. By continuing to follow a B A S W -type strategy, the A C W would at most have remained a spokesman for those few fully qualified community workers employed on a state mediation or corporate patronage basis, ensuring status, salaries, and pension rights comparable with those of social workers.

Restrictive strategies to control the labour market would also involve considerable costs for the A C W. It might have kept unqualified workers out of local government jobs, but it could not have kept them out of community work at a grass-roots level if only because it is quite acceptable, even recognised as admirable, to do it while on social security. Central and local government also tend to adopt a cavalier attitude to the pretensions of 'semi-professions' and appoint non-members to senior posts. Moreover, many marginally employed community workers do enjoy a sort of collegiate professional situation. Certainly their clients don't know what's going on, needs and success are determined by the workers and judged by colleagues (recall those articles in *Community Action*[21] which discuss the lessons to be learnt from the latest failure), and the plethora of *ad hoc* voluntary bodies providing temporary employment exercise relatively little control over what the worker does. Social work has a well-established mainstream and a small radical wing, but community work's relationship with radicalism is far more ambivalent.[22] Although critics see community work as an exercise in social control, there seems little doubt that its hairy radical fringe enjoys much the same glamour among those in the field as do the well-heeled but short-term C D P projects. Neither of these groups of workers is likely to be attracted to an association which insists on long periods of training in return for pension rights.

At a time when community work is changing and developing so rapidly, the sclerosis of professionalisation would have doomed the ACW to a minor role in British community work.

What the ACW can do

The most effective strategy open to the ACW is to respond to the demand for definition by taking on the role of ideological pace-setter; this can be accomplished by taking indirect control of the 'arena'. There will be some competition for this role from CDP and some of the professions interested in community work, but by developing enough overlapping membership, the ACW should have no difficulty in maintaining a focal position. This sort of control might be expected to be accomplished by the following means:

1   Developing credibility as the principal spokesman at a national level is dependent on having a constituency of grass-root workers who are getting results. Naturally, if the majority of the grass-roots members are dispersed and totally occupied at field level throughout the country, they will be able to exert any indirect control by the means suggested here only if there is a central organisation built on the cell principle.

2   By supporting community workers. Redundancy and ingratitude are things that paid community workers are supposed to aim at; long hours and confused work roles things they're supposed to live with; but it helps to have a reference group to encourage and support what you are doing. (Otherwise, of course, you can always take an 'ordinary job' and do community work in your spare time, as most unpaid community workers do. At least one can escape the institutional restraints of employment in that way.) One way of supporting people working in isolated difficult roles is to form cells wherever support is needed. The ACW has made a start in this, and has at least managed to attract to these groups many non-members (including some who have wished to remain so). These should discuss, among other things, changing skills and standards of work. The aim should be to sharpen expertise and to benefit from the best aspects of collegiate professionalism.

3   By arranging regional and national seminars to sharpen the expertise of members and others.

4   By taking the initiative in making visible existing links and by developing other links with radical reform, in the same way that

community work was linked with the civil rights movement in the
USA.

5   By strongly asserting that unpaid community work is as fully
valid an activity as paid community work; by developing schemes to
promote this view publicly.

6   By promoting deliberately an alliance of the sort mentioned
above whereby grass-roots activities—both paid and unpaid—should
join forces with highly trained refugees from middle-class values.

7   By taking the initiative in the educational context. The ACW
should aim for all teachers of community work to be in membership,
and should vigorously solicit the interest and participation of all
students on community work and related courses.

8   By promoting its own literature, which can remedy the dearth
of good training material. This volume is obviously a step in the right
direction.

Conclusion

The underlying assumption of this article has been that the ACW, as
spokesman for the interests of those community workers employed
as social control agents by the bureaucracies, would be doomed as an
influence in the future development of community work, the main
reason for this being that the 'clients' will always suspect this sort of
intervention as tokenistic.[23] The goals of mobilisation, participation
and self-organisation then become marginal values and no one,
including the Home Office, will be convinced that they are getting
any real pay-offs from their sponsored radicalism.

We believe that 'client-centred' community work is desirable and
feasible. The ACW's role as a supportive, evangelistic and dynamic
organisation is to promote such a brand of community work that
reflects developments in the field. Recent changes in ACW policy
indicate that it is beginning, if diffidently, to take on this new role.
For the association to emerge as an ideological pace-setter for
'client-centred' community work, the correct strategy is to provide
the principal forum for debate and to support the informal
relationships by which practising workers maintain self-criticism and
develop their work.

Notes

1 Until 1972, six to nine years' experience had been required, depending on the age of the applicant.
2 See for example: H. M. Vollmer and D. L. Mills (eds), *Professionalisation*, Englewood Cliffs, N.J., Prentice-Hall, 1966, or E. Greenwood, 'Attributes of a profession', *Social Work*, 2 (3), July 1957, pp. 44–55.
3 G. Popplestone, 'The ideology of professional community workers', *British Journal of Social Work*, 1 (1), April 1971, pp. 85–104.
4 H. Wilensky, 'The professionalisation of everyone?', *American Journal of Sociology*, 69, September 1964, pp. 137–58.
5 R. Bucher and A. Strauss, 'Professions in process', *American Journal of Sociology*, 66, January 1961, pp. 325–34.
6 Popplestone, op. cit.
7 We used Popplestone's categories (except that we added an extra one for clergy), but used our interpretation of them. The total membership of 350 is expressed in percentages, with Popplestone's percentages in parentheses:

Social development	3		(6)	
Councils of Social Service	14		(28)	
Administrative posts:		40		61
Voluntary	10		(21)	
Statutory	16		(12)	
Grass roots	30		(12)	
Academics and trainers	15		(12)	
CROs	2		(4)	
Settlements	1		(2)	
Students	6		(4)	
Clergy	2		–	
Unclassified	1		–	

8 Source: ACW Council Minutes.
9 Popplestone, op. cit., pp. 88–89.
10 T. J. Johnson, *Professions and Power*, Macmillan, 1972.
11 For example W. J. Goode, 'Community within a community: the professions', *American Sociological Review*, 22, April 1957, pp. 194–200.
12 Greenwood, op. cit.
13 See A. Etzioni, *The Semi-Professions and their Organisation: Teachers, Nurses and Social Workers*, New York, Free Press, 1969, or W. J. Goode, 'The librarian: from occupation to profession?', *Library Quarterly*, 31, October 1961, pp. 306–18.
14 For example see G. Ritzer and H. M. Trice, *An Occupation in Conflict: A Study of the Personnel Manager*, Ithaca, N.Y., 1969; J. Purvis, 'Schoolteaching as a professional career', *British Journal of Sociology*, 24 (1), 1973, pp. 43–57.
15 Popplestone, op. cit.; C. Cannan, 'Social workers: training and professionalism', in T. Pateman (ed.), *Counter Course: A Handbook for Course Criticism*, Penguin Educational Special, 1972, pp. 247–63.
16 I. Epstein, 'Professionalisation, professionalism, and social worker radicalism', *Journal of Health and Social Behavior*, 9, March 1969, pp. 67–77; I.

Epstein, 'Specialisation, professionalisation and social worker radicalism: a test of the "process" model of the profession', *Applied Social Studies*, 2, 1970, pp. 155–63.

7 Epstein (1970), p. 162.

8 Op. cit.

9 See Philip Bryers in K. Jones (ed.), *The Year Book of Social Policy in Britain 1972*, Routledge & Kegan Paul, 1973, pp. 212–27.

20 John Benington, 'Community work as an instrument of institutional change', in *Lessons from Experience,* report of ACW Annual Conference, 1972.

21 Bimonthly magazine published by Community Action, P.O. Box 665, London SW1X 8DZ.

22 An ambivalence exposed unmercifully in T. Wolfe, *Radical Chic and Mau-Mauing the Flak Catchers,* New York, Bantam Books, 1971.

23 H. Beynon, *Working for Ford*, Penguin, 1973, clearly illustrates working-class suspicion ('They're bent') of even those trade union officials promoted from the shop floor.

6 Some difficulties in introducing a community work option into social work training

George Goetschius

It may be of interest to others introducing a community work option into a traditionally casework course to know of some of the problems it might entail. Although particular circumstances will differ, it is more than likely that some of the same problems will prevail. The 'initiator' should be prepared for this, and not see the problems as peculiar to his situation but as integral to the process of introducing the new option.

The difficulties listed here are not seen as extraneous to the work but work itself.

The following is an outline of some of the difficulties I encountered in developing the community work option and in the orientation of staff and supervisors.

As more professional training courses introduce a community work option (theory and placement), we will doubtless get to know more about the problems and difficulties of doing so. Two years' experience suggested a number of difficulties to me which I will outline, hoping they may suggest one of the bases for discussion among people doing the same or similar job . . . and social work teaching staff facing the same problems. Although some are specific to this situation, most, I think, will occur where the attempt is made to introduce a community work option.

The following list is not in any particular order.

1 *The concept of the individual as basic to casework 'ideology'*

It is extremely difficult for caseworkers who have based their practice on a concept of the individual (Protestant middle class) as an entity, and their treatment process on an exclusive relationship with an individual, to understand and accept that participation in a community venture can lead to individual growth and development.

They tend to focus on the individual to the exclusion of his social role in the performance of tasks. They fear that the community worker is not giving enough attention to the individual, not recognising that the participation itself is the remedial relationship. Thus they tend to define social work as a kind of applied psychology and the client as in need of treatment, whereas in community work most participants are seen as normal, and the personality growth is through performance of tasks, not the worker–client relationship.

2 *Human growth and development teaching*

Human growth and development teaching has traditionally been the backbone of casework teaching and is usually heavily psychoanalytically oriented, with the social dimension often completely lacking. In addition (despite declaimers to the contrary), it often is more concerned with maladjustment and deviance than 'normal' functioning. Even when it covers 'normality and maturity', it often is not able to explain the origin of these value-judgments, which are taken to be biological or psychological givens. Little or nothing is said about how people learn about co-operative or conflict behaviour, about the effect of social institutions, social arrangements on behaviour, etc. What is needed for a truly generic approach is the social psychology of human growth and behaviour.

3 *The limitations of social models presented*

Because casework was the basic discipline, the models presented, whether Freudian learning theory or behaviourism, are seen to deal with the behaviour of individuals. Little is said about groups, and almost nothing about social institutions (the state, school, industry, etc.); but although casework tends to recognise conflict in the individual (and works towards its reconciliation), no modes are present which are relevant to conflict (or dissensus) in society, the usual modes presented being either psychological or biological, rarely social. Not only community work teaching (and learning), but generic social work, requires a greater variety of models to compare and select from.

4 *The nature of community work students, and staff response*

The community work student is already dedicated to participation,

to social change, to questioning the nature of things and the current
set-up (distribution of status, privilege or resources), or he would not
be taking a course to develop his skills to further these aims for client
groups. Naturally he (or she) will apply the same criteria to the
course situation as to work in the field. He is therefore more vocal
about participating in the administration of the course and its
development, and he wishes to practise how to organise to do these
things.

Just as naturally, a staff that is casework-oriented will see a course
problem in terms of individual psychology and attempt to deal with
it in that manner. The community work student will see the
structural aspects of the problem. This is very disturbing indeed to
the continuance of casework course culture.

5 Developing criteria for placements

Although the criteria for a community work placement should be
the same as that for case and group, two points might have to be
considered.

a. Since the community work process is longer than the case or
group process, placements may have eventually to be lengthened in
order to give the student the necessary educational experience of
seeing a project through several of its stages.

b. Whenever possible, a community work placement should be
developed in an area where a casework placement is later possible for
the same student, allowing the student to see (and experience) the
interaction of methods in the same circumstances.

6 The shape of community work practice

Most community work takes place in the evening or at weekends
when the clients have the time to participate, but the worker is
engaged during the day as well in visiting other agencies in
connection with work, meeting with colleagues, preparing for
meetings, etc. This puts more of a strain on the student in a
community work placement than in a case or group one. Time for
reading or class preparation is difficult to arrange. The shape of
community work practice as it relates to student placements should
be carefully looked into.

Mixed placements

The idea of mixed placements in the same agency is not always good, since the division of time and effort tends to either departmentalise the learning experience (case and community work) or cause a conflict in the student about his ultimate responsibility in the placement. To have two supervisors in the same agency may also present a problem. What is needed is two quite separate placements, one case and one group or community, so that a learning experience in depth is possible in both situations. This problem may well solve itself as departments of social service appoint more community workers and mixed placements with the one agency become feasible.

Social action and its political context

Most community work students want to know not only about community development, organisation and care, but about social action as well. Now social action often involves neighbourhood politics (the local council) which, although allowed as a concern to the head of the local department or service, or the profession as a whole (on a national level), is not yet seen to be an ingredient of social work, which has always presented its case as non-political, with the individual worker as strictly non-partisan and, above all, not involved with his clients in anything remotely concerned with the political process. The legitimacy of social action and the acceptance of its political implications is one of the things most resented by caseworkers, yet one of the possible contributions to the development of a truly generic social worker practice.

9 *The difficulties of tutors with a casework orientation*

Tutors with a primary casework orientation find it difficult to accept community work as a mode of social work intervention because they see it as not being directly concerned with individuals (see (1) above), and difficult in the tutorial situation, in that the focus of the learning process of the community work students is based not on the personality of the participants but on the efficiency and effectiveness of their task performance; the role of the worker is thus shifted from a relationship based on concern with individuals to an organisational and task-based one, which requires a change in the focus of the tutor.

10 *Participation, autonomy and power*

Participation, autonomy and power are primary concerns o community workers. The participation of the clients (not in the treatment process but in tasks to do with social change and administration of the agency itself), the challenging of processes and procedures (administrative autonomy) and the nature and content of the decision-making process—the attempt to re-distribute status privilege and resources and the development exercise of the power to do so—are seen from a casework point of view as perhaps outside the preview of social work. This is true only when social work is defined. as it traditionally has been, as casework. Once the generic nature of social work is more fully explored and established, this difficulty will most probably be resolved.

11 *The casework supervisor and the community work dimension*

The same things that are true of the casework-oriented teaching staff are true of the casework supervisors—they tend to be fearful of over-participation of students in the administration of the course, to resent community work students in casework placements pointing out the structural implications of a case (as due to the rigidity or malfunctioning of a social institution or society), and to focus almost entirely on the psychological aspects of the problem. Nor is the community worker's criticism of the processes and procedures of the agency from the point of view of client satisfaction always appreciated. This may well change as more community work students do casework placements, and with a change in staff attitudes.

12 *The generic contradictions*

The generic approach claims that all modes of social work intervention have a common knowledge, understanding and value base, and that even the basic skills are common to the various methods. If this is so (or believed to be so), why is casework still seen as the fundamental discipline, since in generic theory it is simply *one expression* of the same helping process? If you can learn all you need to know about theory and practice in two casework placements, why not two group, residential care, or community work placements? The answer is not that we do not know enough yet about the other methods, but is that (a) the psycho-social is still interpreted as psychological and (b) the idea of 'the individual' (see 1) above) still permeates social work thinking.

13 Difficulties of timetable and administration

Some of these difficulties are not theoretical or ideological, but simply a question of timetable. There is too much to fit into too short a time. The answer here is only three basic lecture courses: 1. Individual behaviour, 2. group behaviour and 3. institutional behaviour: a wider variety of shorter lecture courses, seminars and group discussions which cover a much wider variety of social work concerns, such as social work values and ethics, social control and social change, modes of intervention, the social services, with students making their own choices.

14 The phases of a community project as a placement difficulty

Most community work projects pass through phases: contacting the community, group, building an organisation, planning and carrying out an action sequence, etc. Unlike case or group work agencies, a community work project may accomplish its task and move on, or 'close shop'. This means that unlike case and group work placements, the course may always have to be in the process of developing new placements and allow adequate time for this.

15 The limitations on acceptable placements

Community work is applicable in a wide variety of settings, some of which, although they implement social welfare values, are not traditional social work agencies. This presents a problem, since a local council of churches, a local council housing department or an industrial development board are all settings in which students could learn much (and possibly contribute). Physical and social planning, social agency administration, social work research, etc. are all fields that have excellent placement possibilities and which, if community work is to develop, need to be used. But this cannot be done until more staff and supervisor interpretation (a) transforms the concept of 'the individual' into that of the person, (b) spells out in detail the implication of the concept of the psycho-*social* and (c) further develops the idea of generic social work.

16 *Lack of social agency administration dimension in training*

Because of the casework bias, a good part of the curriculum i
concerned with the individual and his needs, dynamics an
individual, and very little with institutional behaviour. For th
community work (or institutional behaviour), residential care, socia
agency administration student, the nature of institutiona
administrative and bureaucratic behaviour is of equal importance
since these provide the setting in which he will be trying to hel
individuals and groups. Much more information is needed abou
these subjects to balance out the psychiatric orientation (for thos
who want it).

17 *When the agency itself is the target for change (loyalty)*

In community work, it sometimes happens that the agency itself i
the target for change; either its conditions of service, programme o
service or administrative process and procedures may be seen by th
client group as in need of modification or change. Traditiona
casework ideology has put so high a premium on loyalty to th
employing agency (which almost elevates it to a social work value
that the thought of a worker organising a client group against hi
employing agency is either not understood, disapproved of, or i
seen as disloyalty to the employing body.

18 *The fear of a split between community work and other modes o social work intervention*

For some of the reasons outlined here—social action and politics, the
ideology of the individual, the community work concern with
participation, autonomy and power, the agency itself as the
target—some caseworkers feel community work not to be really a
method of social work. By this attitude, by their unwillingness to
change traditional opinions and outlooks, and by constantly harking
back to these differences—which community workers on the whole
find reconcilable—the danger of a split between community work
and other modes of intervention is occasioned. Although, because of
the developing awareness of the generic bases of all modes of
intervention, I doubt whether this will happen, should it arise, it
would be only temporary; as social work develops, its community

work dimension will become more apparent, which would occasion reunion, based on generic theory and practice.

19 *The absence of teaching material based on UK experience*

There is a real lack of teaching material in community work which relates to issues in the U K , and very few good case histories; this is why it is important for students to keep fieldwork records, write placement reports and do fieldwork case studies which can be fed back into community work classes as discussion material—most texts are American.

20 *The position of the 'community work initiator' on the staff*

The person attempting to introduce the community work option is at a disadvantage on several counts: (a) in order to do a good staff interpretation job, he has to challenge the cherished opinions and attitudes of caseworkers; (b) in order to keep the spread of placements broad enough to give adequate student choice, he must often make placement suggestions which are received negatively, and so reinforce the very attitudes and opinions he is trying to change; (c) he is considered responsible for the 'disruptive' behaviour of community work students (who naturally bring community work attitudes and opinions in the same way casework students do); (d) he is seen as being either consensus- or conflict-oriented—politically involved, committed to social action (each by turn)—as different aspects of orientation are undertaken. Altogether, a most stimulating experience.

21 *Resentment of the introduction of new terminology*

Because 'ego', 'id', 'superego', 'transference' and the 'unconscious' have been popularised, they are no longer seen as technical terms or concepts within the Freudian frame of reference, but as simple English.

Since community work on the whole deals with a different level of the social process, to which to a large extent psychoanalytic terminology does not apply, the words and concepts of community work (simple as they are)—'locality system', 'client and target system', 'action sequence'—are called 'unwarranted jargon' and are resented, not only because they are seen as novel (or unnecessary), but also because they do not refer to the same entity and process as psychoanalytic language. In short, the language of community work tends to be more sociologically oriented than the psychoanalytical language of casework.

22 *The need for supervision material*

As there is a lack of materials for teaching community work, so there is a similar lack for the development of fieldwork supervision, which to some extent we made good on this course. The questions here are: to what extent will community work supervision share the same basic orientation as case and group work supervision, and also need it?

23 *The community work agencies' need for consultation*

A real difficulty in introducing this kind of option is that, once contact is made with an agency which can offer an acceptable placement, the agency often feels free to use the school contact to seek advice and consultation about the development of its community work programme. Unlike casework agencies where theory and practice is already developed, many community work agencies or programmes are still working out their terms of reference and seek advice and support. On the one hand this is good, since it keeps one in touch with development in the field, but on the other, unless time is allocated for it and other staff realise the size and nature of the commitment, it can be a difficulty.

24 *The projection on to community work of the social change function*

Students, staff and supervisors sometimes project on to community work the social change function that belongs to the whole profession. Not all of community work is concerned with social change. This is a difficulty since it raises expectations of students who then see themselves *only* as agents of social change, and confirms the critical prejudices of non-community workers who then 'think they know what it is all about' (and proceed to approve or disapprove). This situation will change as the BASW takes on more social action for the whole profession.

25 *The lack of clarity in the BASW attitude to professional associations*

The B A S W itself is either unclear, or unwilling to commit itself, on the place of community work in social work practice or in social work education. On the one hand, its journals cover the subject with much sympathy, on the other, there is confusion about full membership for community workers. In addition, the relation of the B A S W to the A C W is far from clear. All this is reflected in the handouts of the Social Work Advisory Service and in the opinions and attitudes of social work teachers and supervisors.

26 *The informal ventures*

More and more of the younger people are finding they cannot work within the 'establishment' and are setting up community work projects outside the formal social agency setting—working part-time at something else or, as in America, going on to supplementary benefits to live like, and with, their clients. In my opinion, ventures of this kind (like early Settlements) will soon be commonplace—but will they be seen as possible educational placements for professional social work training courses?

27 *Specialist versus general practitioner*

The idea of generic social work, which simply means that there is a common knowledge, understanding and value base underlying the various modes of intervention practised in various settings, should not, I believe, be stretched to suggest that every social worker must be a general practitioner. There will always be a need for specialists such as medical, psychiatric or child guidance. A full-time community work job requires not only the application of common social work knowledge, understanding and values, but different skills applied in different circumstances, and is a specialisation.

28 *May students be more committed to one than to the other?*

There appears to be a fear that community work students will be more committed to community work than to case- or group work, but, for some reason, no fear that they will develop casework skills at the expense of community work skills. This is because of the generic contradiction (see (12) above) which still sees casework as the basic discipline. This can work against the community work student who gets a good community work assessment but only a moderate casework assessment, whereas if a community work student gets a good casework assessment and a moderate community work one, all appears to be well.

29 *Community work supervisors still feel a common bond*

To some extent, community work supervisors still feel a common bond, which in the early days of developing placements is a good thing, since it helps in the development and discussion of material for community work supervision. Yet there is a danger that a community work supervisors' group could form within the total body of supervisors; this would prevent them from making an adequate contribution to the general group and they would appear to the general group to be a clique.

30 *The demand for integration too soon*

Although the knowledge, understanding and values of community work are the same as those that underlie the rest of social work, the necessary skills and the circumstances in which the knowledge, understanding and values are applied differ from one mode of intervention to another. This is especially true of community work, which will need for some time to have a community work class (including methods) for the whole year. It is too soon to integrate community work teaching into the course as an undifferentiated item.

31 *The value base of community work*

Because social work is a value based on humanity, there is much concern about whether the values underlying generic social work are the same as those underlying community work. This is usually expressed in relation to (1) above, and is part of the casework fear that 'task' will not produce 'process'. I suspect this will take years of patient discussion on both sides for any real progress to be made.

2 Relations with non-professionals

Community work, at least in its current state of development, appears to be more open to the outside than professional social work. Any over-enthusiastic relations with teachers, youth workers, clergymen or lawyers are suspect as not being related to professional social work. This is not true of relations with doctors—since the medical model is still, by and large, operable, this is permissible. Community work could make a real contribution here by including physical planners, etc.

33 Is community work a con?

Students often ask 'is community work yet another con?'—leading people to believe that they can make decisions which are, in fact, made elsewhere—asking them to perform by self-help tasks what should be performed by the state—giving the illusion of power and participation when in fact they cannot really affect the most vital issue—the redistribution of wealth.

This can be answered only by admitting that community work as a method of social work is limited in its ability to affect the 'whole system' and that the most that can be hoped for is limited gradual change in specific circumstances. But the effects of helping people to act co-operatively to achieve common goals may well have a greater effect than the achievement of the goal itself.

34 Fears about professional identity

Because the community worker tends to see his loyalty as primarily client-based (rather than agency-based), because he is willing to organise against the agency that employs him, and because he tends to be concerned with non-casework skills and talk in a non-casework 'language', there are some who have fears about his professional identity—what they really mean is his casework identity. But as the base of social work practice broadens I doubt the fear will persist. With the incorporation of group work, residential care, social agency administration and research in generic casework, the conceptual frame of reference will spread out and social work will be recognised as more than simply casework.

35 *Social service, social welfare, social work*

There is currently an attempt to separate social service and social
welfare from social work in order to protect and further
'professional' aims and objectives. Considering the basic social
mandate underlying all three, I do not think this is a logical or
honest differentiation. It certainly makes no sense for community
work, social agency administration, residential care, social work
research, however advantageous it might be to protect casework
professionalism. But I doubt, as social work matures, that this
differentiation will be viable. This will be especially true as social
service and welfare workers (on the make for their own
professionalism) develop training programmes which will more and
more overlap and interrelate with current professional training.

Concluding comments

Most of these difficulties require detailed staff discussion over a
long period (say two years), but most are obviated by:
1 The joint staff/student experience of working things out
together.
2 The experience of tutors in tutoring community work students
and visiting placements.
3 The exchange of opinions between staff and the community
work institutor—formally and informally and in staff seminars
which concentrate on community work.

All of these slowly change *both* the attitudes and expectations
of the staff, *and* the ideas and expectations of the initiator. In our
case, most of the issues listed have either been resolved, are being
resolved or are still under discussion.

From what one knows and hears about the past, the problems
listed, although explicitly different, are implicitly similar to those
which arose in the early development of professional training in
casework, the move from the 'settings' approach to casework to
that of generic casework, and the introduction of group work into
generic social work training. They were to be expected, are
amenable to co-operative solution, and are temporary.

As generic social work develops, community work, residential
care, social agency administration, social work research and social
work education will all face similar problems as they are integrated

nto the casework-oriented training situation. But since all share a common mandate, common knowledge and understanding and a common value base, they will each in turn come to be seen as part of the repertoire of modes of intervention of generic social work practice.

7   In-service community work training: a job-centred approach

John Ward

The assumption that full-time training in a college or university is a relevant preparation for community work must be challenged. Few of the leading workers in the field at present have formal community work qualifications received after following a full-time course in an educational institution. In view of the concern felt in community work circles at the insensitivity of agencies to the needs of the communities they serve, it is understandable that the training of the 'professionals' staffing these same agencies and institutions should be regarded with suspicion. Should the job needing to be done determine the nature of the training? Or does the training determine what job is done, whatever the needs? The whole ethos of community work rejects the latter and supports the former view. It follows that the role of the educational institution in training workers must be drastically redefined. The values dominant in most educational institutions (e.g. 'academic excellence', acceptance of teacher–pupil hierarchy, literacy, etc.) have little relevance, indeed can be contradictory, to those found at the field level. Can a worker acquire knowledge, skills and values in a setting so different from the one in which he or she is going to work? Greater emphasis placed on training which builds on the worker's own experience and job situation is required. Experiments in a variety of approaches to the training problems of community workers are needed before resources are allocated to traditional in-institution programmes. The following report describes just one such experiment of an in-service type, where the employing agencies have no say over content and purpose, and the needs of the workers and their community are given priority.

The National Council of Social Service, an organisation concerned to facilitate co-operation between voluntary agencies employing community workers, responded to the urgent need for training by developing a programme of in-service courses with a primary focus on the on-going work of the participants. An experimental course in 1966 led to the development of the present programme. A report was published in 1968.[1] Since January 1970 twelve courses have been run involving 195 participants, of which 95 were employed by voluntary organisations and 100 by statutory authorities. These courses—how they evolved, the thinking behind them—will be described here.

Assumptions and philosophy

The programme began with an assumption that emergency courses would be required only for a *short period*, in fact until such time as the institutional training bodies had adjusted their programmes in order to provide adequate training facilities to meet the growing need for community workers. With this in mind, co-operation was sought with those university departments with appropriate expertise and in a position to assist with short-term initiatives. The fact that the funding all came from outside the universities made full co-operation relatively easy to achieve. Also, we were able to take advantage of the residential accommodation available in the universities and the easier access to experts to lead sessions and act as consultants.

It was believed that there was value to be attached to *regionally based courses* which drew participants and staff from the locality. Hence, courses have been held at the following universities:

York, Department of Social Administration (serving the north-east), 2 courses
Manchester, Department of Adult Education (serving the north-west), 1 course
Liverpool, Department of Extension Studies (serving the north-west), 1 course
Leicester, Department of Adult Education (serving the Midlands area), 4 courses
Exeter, Department of Social Administration (serving the south-west), 1 course
Brunel, Department of Organisation and Social Studies (serving London and south-east), 3 courses

By virtue of these regional bases, it was hoped that the participants would be encouraged to develop a more supportive relationship with one another, and find it easier to draw on the resources of the training institutions even after the course was completed. Further, it was hoped that involvement in these programmes would encourage the universities to develop their own training in community work.

Since most of the literature on community work, until very recently, was drawn from outside England (mainly from America), it was felt that community work would need to develop its own identity on the British scene. Little was yet known about how community work could or should develop in this country. Therefore, an in-service training programme with a primary focus on the participants' on-going work could provide an opportunity for workers to develop a type of community work, in consultation with one another and interested academics, which would most appropriately fit their particular setting. This principle has proved of great importance in the development of the programme. At no point was it assumed that a training programme could take on the traditional aspects of training, with a monopoly of knowledge and skills on the part of the teachers and the complete absence of the same on the part of the students or participants. We have always started each course on the assumption that everyone, teachers and students, have something to give and something to get from the course.

Community work philosophy has obviously informed much of the thinking about the course structure and content. Every effort has been made to make the course methods consistent with community work practice. Increasing emphasis has been placed on using fully the resources and skills represented by the participants themselves in the learning situation. We have practised in the training situation what we preach as community workers, and have become convinced that this method of approach is a more appropriate way of meeting training needs in community work than the traditional in-institution approach.

Because the responsibility of in-service training in community work within the National Council of Social Service rests with a training department which also has responsibility for staff training and development programmes within the voluntary movement as a whole, the courses were influenced by aspects of modern thinking in the training and organisation development field. In particular, the concept of 'training need' as the short-fall between the requirements of a job and what a person brings to that job in terms of knowledge, skills and values found a very special relevance in the context of the courses. The levels of experience, knowledge, skills and values which each participant brought to the course were as wide as were the variety of settings from which they came, so that it was almost impossible to provide a basic course, in the traditional form, which would have met anything more than a small proportion of their needs. What clearly was needed was a course framework to help individual participants to identify their particular training needs and to provide them with the resources to meet those needs—if possible from within the course, if not, from elsewhere. Hence, for some, the courses proved most significant only as a first step in a programme of self-education.

Considering it is a norm in community work practice to challenge the relevance and efficiency of service delivery by institutions and organisations in the community, it is not surprising that the course framework has never been permitted by participants, or, indeed some staff, to settle into anything resembling an institutional mould providing ritualised training in some quasi-religious community work dogma. By trying to start where participants are in terms of serving their community, the course has been able to avoid some of the major weaknesses of the in-institution training programmes, in particular the danger of losing touch with the felt needs of the client system or community of reference and developing 'rules' of practice largely irrelevant to those needs and the real situation in which they exist.

Participants

The participants are drawn from a wide range of settings. On most courses, *about* half the participants were employed by voluntary organisations and half by statutory agencies, as was indicated above. This was a deliberate act of policy on our part. We believe that a valuable part of such a course is the interchange of experience between participants; thus people working in settings as different as between voluntary and statutory agencies can particularly benefit from being together in a learning situation.

The origins of the participants in terms of the institutions employing them is also of interest in making up an 'ideal mix' for a course. We prefer to draw from a variety of settings including social work, education, planning, housing and church-based workers. Such is the nature of the present development of community work in this country that the majority seeking training now come from the social service field (about 50 per cent), with education making up the second biggest group (about 25 per cent). Recently, community workers have come forward who are not employed within one of the main institutions such as social work or education, and who see themselves, and indeed are viewed by their employers, as members of a community work discipline which owes primary allegiance to no other. It remains to be seen whether this phenomenon will increase.

The vast majority themselves choose whether to come on the course, and request their employers to second them as appropriate. However, a few are ordered by their employers to attend. This latter group, in the early stages of the courses, were to prove difficult. They came feeling resentful that their employers believed they needed further training, and determined to prove that this 'thing called community work' was no different from their own main discipline, or that it was irrelevant to the needs of communities as they saw them, or that it was left-wing radicalism thinly disguised as professional practice!

The ages have ranged widely from twenty-one to fifty-eight. The majority have been under thirty-five. The numbers of men and women are approximately equal. Their experience and seniority have also varied, but a significant number of the more senior staff come from statutory agencies where they have been given specific briefs to develop community work practice within their departments.

Planning the course

The planning starts with the recruitment of the key staff who will act as director or joint directors. Then accommodation for the residential periods is booked and the recruitment of participants begins. The formal course content is minimal, as will be seen in the later descriptions, but usually arrangements are put in hand to forewarn the 'experts' that they might be invited to contribute to the course either as session leaders or consultants. The course proper begins with an introductory day seminar when the objectives of the course are discussed in some detail with the participants, their expectations of the course are solicited, their opinions about the course structure sought and agreement about the initial arrangements reached. From this point onwards, the planning of the course is a joint enterprise.

The appointment of the *course director*, or of *joint directors*, is undertaken by the N C S S . The course director then arranges the details described above, including approaching a number of persons to act as consultants to individual participants, if required. (A recent suggestion has been that course directors should see themselves as acting as community workers, and work with the participants as if members of an evolving community group with whom they are working towards some educational goal. This would offer an exciting prospect of the whole course taking on an even more dynamic form, providing opportunities for carefully monitored practical experience within the course situation as well as 'at work'.)

Course structure

As in most other community work situations, a certain amount of organisation is useful to make the best use of the available resources of time, participants' experience and commitment, and outside experts, and to provide a context for growth and development. The course has three main components (1) working in groups on day seminars and residential periods, (2) individual projects, and (3) individual consultations.

Most courses span a period of approximately four months. They involve at least ten days in residence, usually five days at the initial stage and five at the end. An introductory day seminar is held about a month before the first residential period and other day seminars (up to three) are held at intervals between the two residential periods. One course has experimented in holding a two-day residential seminar instead. Participants are asked to allow one day per week, when back at work, to carry out the course projects. This is the minimum time recommended for participants to carry out the course work. Some, because of the flexibility of their work situation or the immediate relevance of the course to their work, are able to spend a lot more time.

The prime objective of *working in groups* is to begin the process of identifying the knowledge, skill, values and assumptions on which community work is based, and to contrast these with the work situation of the participants themselves. Through this, it is hoped that they will begin to recognise their own training needs and begin to utilise the resources available on the course to meet them. These include the experts on hand, films and other aids, reading material and the experience and knowledge of other participants.

The second component—*individual projects*—is designed to

sharpen the awareness of the actual demands of the participant's present job and to identify ways in which demands might be more satisfactorily met. Here, two exercises are involved: a 'job analysis' aimed to give an opportunity of looking at the participants' own particular job situations, and a 'project analysis' to assess a piece of work with which they are immediately concerned, giving particular attention to the information and skills they need to carry it through successfully.

The third component is the provision of an *individual consultant* to each participant with the brief to support and help him or her to achieve the training objectives. Much depends on the quality of the relationship which develops, but the focus tends to be initially on the 'job analysis' and subsequently on the 'project analysis'. All consultants are expected to spend at least one session in the participant's own work environment.

The working in groups period includes a minimum of ten days of intensive work in residence. Since major emphasis is placed on groups and group processes very early in the programme, participants are introduced to the theory and practice of working with groups. The practice continues for the duration of the course. Role-playing exercises have been used on all courses and simulation games are increasingly being used.

Films have proved useful: the Alinsky films made by the National Film Board of Canada have been particularly relevant and stimulating. Recently, sessions using video television have been developed. Training aids are in the form of short excerpts from publications in the programme. During the residential periods, a book box is kept which contains most of the recommended reading. However, it is assumed that fieldworkers, faced with the same kinds of pressures as the majority of participants, will not be able to do a great deal of reading, although every encouragement is given for participants to make full use of the reading available.

A model of a 'job analysis' which has recently been used on one of the courses is included at the end of this chapter. These guides are usually given out on the first day introductory seminar, and the participant is expected to have completed this or a similar job analysis by the first day of the residential period. Three copies are asked for: one for the participant, one for the course director and one for the consultant. It is a matter for the participant to decide whether to discuss the job analysis with fellow participants. It should be noted at this point that participants are asked to observe

he confidential nature of some of the information they will be
given. This can be important, especially for those who are anxious to
discuss frankly difficult job situations which are inhibiting them
from moving forward in their real work.

Under no circumstances does the course director provide a
participant's employer with a report on him or her. A formal *letter
of recognition* that a participant attended the course, and completed
the projects, is sent on request, both to the participant and, if
necessary, to the employer, once it is over. The only conditions for
issuing this formal letter are that the participant does attend the
working in group sessions and completes (to his or her own
satisfaction) the two projects.

The job analysis is used by the course director and the participant
as a means of assessing training needs. In discussion with the course
director and the consultant, it is possible to identify the
opportunities and obstacles experienced by the worker. It is not
unusual for participants to have a community work brief and yet be
so constrained by their setting as to make it almost impossible for
them to carry it out. On occasions, the job analysis has been
discussed extensively with employers and colleagues, and indeed has
in a few cases become the means by which major improvements in
the work situation have been achieved.

The project analysis requires the participants to choose a piece of
work with which they are presently involved and describe the nature
of their involvement, linking this with a careful analysis of what they
need to know about their community in order successfully to carry
this project forward. This project combines the elements of a
community study with a process report on activities relevant to the
development of the work. By subjecting a piece of work to this
careful analysis, it is hoped, with the support of the consultant, to
increase the possibilities for a successful outcome in the project to
some extent, as well as to allow for learning through experience, in
the process.

To provide the participant with an individual consultant is
probably the unique feature of this course. So isolated are
community workers from their professional colleagues, so
demanding is the work, that there has always been an urgent need for
them to have a network of consultants for support and help. In an
ideal situation, workers and academics involved in this field should
be able to provide a sufficient network to meet all needs through
mutual support and help. However, with the present position of

knowledge and skills and the real shortage of experienced workers, is necessary to fit these consultations into a fairly short time, i.e. the four months of the in-service course. The consultants are selected for their experience and knowledge of the field, are generally sympathetic and supportive, and in no way act as supervisors. Every effort is made to avoid a consultant being in any way connected with the participant's organisation or hierarchy. They are asked to visit the participant at least once in the job situation and to spend time with the worker in looking at the area served. For the duration of the course, consultant and participant maintain contact both on the telephone and in face-to-face sessions. Consultants are kept closely informed of the course programme and, indeed, some are invited in to give sessions on the residential courses. There has never been difficulty in recruiting them, although they are not generously paid and very often put in a great deal more time than has been asked of them, continuing in a supporting relationship with the participant well after the completion of the course. The academics who are used as consultants have commented on how useful they find the experience in keeping them in touch with the field, and the fieldworkers who have been similarly involved claim to have gained some useful insights from the experience. The success or failure depends very much on the rapport which is established; clearly, from our experience, when it does work, it works very well indeed, and some of the comments of participants indicate that this was the most valuable part of the course for them.

The matching of participant and consultant is done by the course director(s) in consultation with the two individuals involved. The training need of the participant is the ideal criterion, rather than some concept of personal compatibility. The relationship between them is essentially temporary, but it is recognised that the director in exercising discretion in 'arranging a marriage' between consultant and participant is acting somewhat arbitrarily. The difficulty of any other method is discussed openly, and participants are asked if they think that the arrangements might be completed by other means. So far, participants have unanimously agreed to leave it to the discretion of the course director—which always comes as a slight surprise. The consultant is invited to the last day of the first residential period in order to receive the papers relating to the consultee, discuss any problems with the course director(s) and meet the participant over drinks and lunch.

Attempts are made to maintain a steady feedback on the courses

By allowing considerable scope for self-programming, there is a tendency for evaluation to precede decisions about the next part of the programme, so within the course itself there is fairly immediate evaluation. However, this is not always very relevant. In terms of the actual learning achieved, efforts are made in a final session of the course to get a broader view, when the group is asked whether expectations have been realised or not. Subsequently, about a month after the end of the course, a brief open-ended questionnaire is sent to participants to elicit their further comments and evaluation.

A few have not completed the course. Most commonly they have not been able to finish the project analysis. Their evaluation tends to indicate that they felt too much was expected of them by the course, and that not enough allowance was made for work problems. It should be noted that one of the conditions for accepting participants is that they will be allowed (or will allow themselves) one day a week off from their routine work in order to carry out the projects. This has not meant that they were not working directly for the agency, but it did relieve them from continual involvement in the daily grind, with time to reflect and consider their position more objectively. Those who found the course either difficult or impossible tended to be unable to negotiate such a position for themselves. In several cases, in the view of the course director and the consultant, inability to complete the course directly resulted from what could only be described as 'impossible work conditions'. This was true of both voluntary and statutory employers. Fortunately, only a few participants experienced this problem, but without the consultants, we believe that many more would have had to face similar difficulties.

While the greater majority of the participants believe that they benefited in some way from the in-service programme, the nature of their progress varied, as would be expected, since their needs varied. A common view was their enjoyment of the course and the pleasure they derived from being with like-minded people for a period. Almost all felt they had a better understanding of community work and its place in their work, while some believed their practical skills had been extended and developed by the course.

Many of the staff, in particular the directors, find the courses useful in developing their sensitivity to the developments in the community work field, a point of view echoed by the consultants. The courses are very demanding for the directors, because although the structure is somewhat similar in each course, the actual content, reflecting the variation in participants, is always different. Organising courses can be exciting and stimulating, but is always very exhausting.

Little attempt has been made, so far, to check on the views of the agencies sponsoring the participants. If requests for 'more of the same' is any guide, we can only assume that they are satisfied. It is perhaps a reflection on the courses' attitude that attention should be mainly given to the needs of the participants and the community they serve rather than to fulfilling the expectations of employers. While we are able to pursue this philosophy, we believe better training can be achieved.

One main conclusion drawn from the experience so far leads one to question fundamentally the appropriateness of basing community work training in formal educational settings using traditional educational methods. Our initial view of the training as merely an emergency programme has changed to a conviction that training which starts with the focus on the worker's job, and then draws in the training resources as appropriate or relevant, is a superior method. It follows that we should recognise that 'training need' is a function of every work situation and that training must be seen as a continuous process spanning the worker's whole career, whatever the setting or whatever the seniority.

The experience leaves me with a conviction that the approach to training of community workers must itself be guided by, and consistent with, community work knowledge, skills and values in order to be fully effective. This is necessary if it is to become flexible enough to meet the ever-changing patterns of needs faced by the communities in which we work.

Guidelines for the job analysis

The purpose of the job analysis is to encourage the individual worker to re-examine in an objective manner certain aspects of his work and that of his agency. The exercise involves looking at three main areas: the structure of the agency and its relationship to its external environment, the worker's relationship to his agency and the relationship of the worker in the agency to individual clients and groups. Thus we can begin to assess goals, resources, methods and their relation to each other, and the problem posed to you when discrepancies occur.

1. *Description of employing agency*
   a) Brief statement of formal aims and objects of the agency. This may be found in constitutions, annual reports or in legislation.
   b) The structure of the agency. Organisational charts may show this. Try to give numbers of staff at appropriate levels.
   c) Give the position of those to whom you are (a) immediately responsible, and (b) ultimately responsible.
   d) Describe your governing committee. Note such points as sex, age, politics or special interests of members. Define how they are appointed.
   Advisory committees should be treated as above.
   e) Describe the geographical area of responsibility. Note any groups for whom you have special responsibilities either legislatively or by agency tradition, etc. Contacts with other agencies, e.g. joint programmes or initiatives.
   f) Any further comments on such factors as differences between formal and informal aims of the agency, the appropriateness of the structure for the achievement of objects, conflicts between objectives of field staff and those of administrative staff, etc. Conflicts with other agencies.

2. *Description of your work*
   a) State briefly your terms of employment and explain your long and short term objectives as you see them. Note such factors as areas of conflict between professional and administrative tasks, delegation of authority, conflicts of role, special responsibilities, etc.
   b) Give a description of the environment you work in, note contacts with other agencies, e.g. voluntary bodies, statutory bodies, central or national organisations. Note areas of conflict, co-operation and overlap. Examine the role of such functions as PR, fundraising, etc.

3. *Relationship with 'clients' and/or community groups*
   a) How are 'clients' and/or community groups and agency brought together?
   b) How much of your work is concerned with the following functions:-
      (i) Grievance solving with organisations and individuals;
      (ii) Information gathering in respect of job;
      (iii) Information giving to groups, individuals and organisations;

(iv) Committee work, including co-ordination of other
agencies around problems, identifying needs, etc;
(v) Involvement in the political process.

NB We are not so much concerned with amounts of time in this section but rather the priorities given to these tasks. These priorities may vary over time and from agency to agency depending on their orientation and traditions.

4. To help with the above analysis we suggest you keep a diary of professional tasks for one week. This should include interviews with individuals and groups, contacts with groups, assistance rendered, etc.

5. Any further comments which you feel are relevant to your analysis and which are not covered in the guidelines.

Reference

1 R.A.B. Leaper, *Community Work*, National Council of Social Service, London, 1968.

Part III Work in Progress/ Developments in the Field

8 Grapevine: an experimental project in community sex education

Janet Evanson and Iain Watkinson

'Resentment, apathy, mistrust—the dead-end jobs—a rejection of the values of adult society'[1] is as true today of a large group of young people as it was when written about the unattached in 1965. Add to this a complex society of multi-standards and it is small wonder that young people who have little or no contact with sympathetic and knowledgeable adults are often confused, misinformed, myth-ridden and misrepresented in matters of sexuality and personal relationships. What is still a taboo subject in many homes rubs shoulders uneasily with the intrusive sexual ambivalence of the mass media, which implies, on the one hand, that sexual intercourse should be confined to a loving and caring relationship—and let that be marriage—yet, on the other, appears to be recommending uninhibited and carefree coupling.

It is a paradox that in 1973, the year in which the school-leaving age was raised to sixteen, there should be so many young people leaving school lacking a sound knowledge of human physiology and sexual development, who probably also will have had no opportunity for informed and frank discussion about relationships either at school or in the home which would help them to come to terms with their own sexuality and to be more understanding of the expectations and emotional needs of their sexual partners. Blocked by embarrassment at appearing sexually naive and by their mistrust of 'the system', they seldom seek the information they need from the specialist agencies and are vulnerable to many a personal crisis at a time of sexual experimentation. The pressures of their peers to conform to the overt mores of the group also contribute to the misconceptions which young people have about each other's real needs and actual sexual behaviour. It is assumed that everybody else knows about sex and birth control, and it takes a brave spirit to admit ignorance or innocence.

The situation in Britain in 1972-3 can be summarised as follows:

Statistics[2] showed a rising trend in the number of abortions, shotgun weddings, illegitimate births and cases of V D among teenagers and the under-sixteens.

Too many parents feel ill prepared or uncomfortable in broaching the subject of sexuality and birth control with their children; a repeating pattern of inadequate sex education by one generation of the next must be broken.

Sex and health education in schools is uneven in quality; many do not even attempt it.

Up to the present time, training for teachers and youth and community workers includes nothing on how to put across sex education; again, many workers are not aware of the relevant sources available to them.

Many young people pick up their information on sex from school friends who may themselves be grossly misinformed; there is no easy and informal way of checking the facts.

Publicity campaigns have yet to prove their influence with the unattached, who reject the 'establishment' values associated with many of the counselling and clinic services on offer.

It was against this background that Grapevine was launched in July 1972, appearing to some to be a surprisingly 'alternative' child to spring from its august parent, the Family Planning Association, but recognisable as a chip off the old block to those versed in the history of the early campaigners for birth control. Grapevine has been set up as an experimental action/research project with the aims of making sex education, in the widest sense, available and acceptable to sexually active young people, including the socially disadvantaged and ethnic minority groups. A report on the first two years' work will include an independent evaluation by the Institute of Education, London.

The personal approach

A basic assumption of Grapevine is that the personal approach is the one most likely to prove effective in sex education and that young people should undertake this work themselves, after training and with the support of professional workers. One obvious advantage of this way of working is that it capitalises on the spontaneity of social interaction between young people and reduces the problems which differences in status can bring to communications. Furthermore, provided the group of voluntary workers is broad-based and reasonably representative of local young people, it serves as a filter in sifting out some of the more middle-class jargon of sex and health education and translates the information and the concepts into the idiom of the community or the sub-culture concerned. Equally important, it brings into Grapevine a many-faceted view of how local young people see their world, and hard data on what proportion of those contacted express a need for specific types of information or assistance, and how this need is met.

The young volunteers who have worked with Grapevine in the first year believe in adopting an honest and open approach to sex, and the many discussions held in the course of their training help them to see that the best approach is to be responsive to the 'needs' which other young people express—for information, befriending, support through a crisis—rather than to go out with a prepared message and the presumption that it is right to tell other people what they should do in the area of personal relationships. In the past, sex education has shown a tendency to separate sexuality and any hint of sexual pleasure from a somewhat clinical view of how male and female develop physiologically and reproduce themselves. In other words, teaching about birth control and venereal disease has been so bound up with sexual intercourse and spacing children within marriage that relevance to love-making among the young unmarried has been obscured.

Detached youth work has nearly always been the province of the professional. Grapevine contends that an intelligent merging of professional leadership and support with the energy, creativity and diversity of a large group of young volunteers drawn from the community can be vastly more effective in making contact with the young unattached than the lone detached worker who is only too frequently without adequate personal support. This contention has been put to the test in the first year and it has been found that young people can indeed be just as effective contact workers, mixing as they do quite naturally in the places where the young congregate—the discos, public houses, adventure play-grounds, markets, the street—and making contacts which may lead on to discussions about relationships, sex, venereal disease, birth control and related topics. Between peers, these subjects can be talked about naturally, without embarrassment or pressure—as easily and informally as football or the music scene.

The use of social interaction for the exchange of ideas and information is not new but, so far as is known, there is as yet no widely recognised form of training which is suited to a group of young people who have selected themselves on the basis of interest in Grapevine's work and who encompass a wide range of social class, educational attainment, skills, attitudes, political beliefs and motivation. To be prepared to talk to strangers about sex in public, a worker—whether professional or amateur—needs to be relatively secure and supported. How can this be achieved? Too much preparation can be unhelpful in that it builds up inhibition and saps spontaneity, yet it would be irresponsible to throw young people into this work without first giving them the opportunity to inform themselves and to clarify some of their own doubts and perplexities. The evolution of training within Grapevine has been interesting and is a continuous process.

Workshop basic training

The first group of twenty-five volunteers were catalysts drawn from outside the area and they shared with the project staff the main burden of evolving a Grapevine philosophy, group identity and the initial programme of work. No one had attempted anything quite like this before, and it was to some extent a question of trial and error and striking out bravely together. As the project developed and new groups of volunteers were brought in (in all, sixty-three volunteers completed their workshop training in the first year), trainers and volunteers became much clearer about the special difficulties of the task and were able to modify plans accordingly. The modifications were all in the direction of getting volunteers out more quickly into the community so that they could learn by observation and by being drawn into social contact with other Grapevine workers who were already accepted in that particular pub or club. With the first group there had been greater emphasis on role play and imaginary case presentations, but it has been found that there is no substitute for first-hand experience, provided that support is available at the time (from the field officers). Learning can occur either in the pub or later in group discussion with a counsellor.

An early lesson was that, on the basis of self-selection, not every volunteer felt comfortable or confident enough to work in a large musical pub, so other work situations had to be selected. Some of the volunteers chose to work in the Centre on the telephone information service, while others visited local youth clubs, adventure playgrounds and a street market. Other alternatives have now been developed, as it is recognised that pub work is probably the most demanding; on the other hand, those who are good at it do find it fun, and working as a group in a specific work situation engenders a feeling of camaraderie and support.

Preparing workers for an unstructured situation creates training problems even where the trainee meets some specified level of qualification and is available on a full-time basis for a year or more. For Grapevine, the problems are considerable, as each incoming group of intending volunteers is available only at weekends and on certain evenings, has joined the project for a wide variety of personal reasons and is seeking unspecified job satisfaction. First of all, they spend a Saturday together in which they see films, meet a family planning doctor and have innumerable discussions about their attitudes to sex education, Grapevine and life in general. For the next two to three weeks, they come into the Centre one or two evenings a week for work in groups of eight to ten volunteers, and explore personal reactions—insights and uncertainties—which are directly linked to the work to be done and the conditions of work. At the end of this workshop period, another whole Saturday is spent by the whole group together in comparing their experiences and probably making some work commitments for the future. By any standards, this is a very brief basic training for a situation in which a volunteer may be asked for very much more than straight information. The balance seems to be struck by placing newly trained volunteers in work groups with more experienced workers, teaching them to draw on each other's skills and those of the professional worker when in doubt, and making it obligatory for any volunteer doing contact work to attend the regular grou training meetings for his particular work group. By building u group support and friendships within Grapevine, there is som insurance against the depressing effects of occasional rejection b the 'client' or the more subtly demoralising discovery tha preventive health and sex education, at the level of givin information without any feedback as to whether or how it will b used, is not sufficiently emotionally satisfying after a while.

At this stage, some of the volunteers may begin to doub whether there are in fact many problems around and can los heart quickly unless the next stage of training is seen to b relevant to overcoming the communication barrier which sometimes prevents young people from saying what is really troubling them. At the time of writing, a case presentation grou is about to be set up which will be led by a counsellor and will a first comprise only a small number of volunteers, those most likely to take up youth or social work in due course. It is hoped that once the benefits are recognised, it will then be possible to set u more than one such group.

It will be seen that Grapevine is essentially a team approacl which enables young people to play a full part in the planning and decision-making process of a group which eventually will be up to 100 active volunteers at any one time. The sixty-three volunteers who have completed their workshop training worked with the project for some months at least. It is too soon to say what the average length of service is likely to be, and some volunteers who are interested in learning to work at a deeper level than straight information will probably stay for some time. To date there is no clear pattern emerging as to the reasons why volunteers retire, but this is an area which will be discussed in our final report. As Grapevine recruits on a self-selection basis as a matter of principle, it is accepted that a number will inevitably find after a while that the work is not for them, but at least they will take away with them the benefit of their training and work experience.

The support currently available to the volunteers is two field officers (the Youth/Community Officer and the Voluntary Work Organiser), a number of part-time counsellors, most of whom are prepared to go out into the pubs and work alongside the volunteers, the Project Manager and the External Supervising Consultant. The first group are all in the age range twenty-five to thirty-five and are directly involved in the community work, while

he latter are more concerned with an overview of the project's
rogress at any one time and in helping the team improve its
erformance and to plan wisely.

he task

rapevine's mission then, is to make contact with those young
eople who will not, of their own volition, reach professional
ources of help (even though their need may be very great) and to
ct as a befriending and bridging organisation.

In general, it is concerned with normal young people whose
ain need is for reliable information and friendly contact with
ther young people with whom they can discuss current
ifficulties and needs. It may be helpful to set out the main
ategories into which we see our 'clients' falling in operational
erms:

Young people wanting straight information about birth control,
v d , sexuality, accommodation, jobs, etc.

Young people wanting befriending, help in making relationships
with the opposite sex, discussion of promiscuity, morality, etc.

Young people with some temporary crisis, most of whom
probably need a sympathetic listener, factual information and
personal support over a short period. Much of this can be done
by volunteers suitably supported by counsellors and staff.

Young people who suspect that they may be abnormal in some
way in their ability to relate to others and are deeply concerned
about this or some other aspect of their functioning.

A minority who appear to be disturbed and in need of
psychiatric assessment.

In the first seven months of community work, the volunteers
were operating largely at the level of categories 1, 2 and 3 but, as
confidence has grown and the in-service training has been
developed in ways which are more closely tailored to specific work
situations, there is a greater readiness and wish, on the part of

some individuals, to work at a deeper level. In the first year most counselling cases arose independently of the volunteers, either in response to an advertisement in *Time Out* or directly to a field officer or counsellor.

At the time of writing, therefore, we have still to show that the team approach in the community—volunteer contact workers fanning out, supported by field officers and counsellors—is able to function effectively in the category 4–5 level. The question is twofold: what proportion of young people met in the community fall into categories 4–5 and, second, what proportion of the volunteers wish to develop their skills so that these deeper problems can emerge? The usual pattern is for a group of four to six volunteers to work in a given situation on a regular basis accompanied on most occasions by a field officer or counsellor for at least some of the time. A well balanced team might include a sixteen-year-old (some of whom are excellent at making the first contact), one or two less experienced volunteers and two or three volunteers who may not find it so easy to make the initial contact but are good listeners and can talk easily about the things that really matter to them or the other person. These are the workers who are more likely to receive confidences and who will increasingly make more use of the counselling support and the newly set up case presentation group. In the case of category 4 clients, it will usually be possible for volunteer and counsellor to work as a pair, the amount of responsibility carried by the volunteer varying with the circumstances; at the very least, the volunteer can continue with befriending.

If indeed this proves a successful method of identifying the deeper problem areas, then the Grapevine model would presumably be of interest from the point of view of preventive mental health work in the community, as well as for its original purpose. Reliable information which is easily accessible can, in many cases, forestall a problem, as the following example illustrates. A recently-joined male volunteer aged twenty was approached at work by a young man who was much concerned about his genitals, which he believed to be outsized as he could not find a sheath large enough. It was discovered that he was ignorant of the first rule of putting on a sheath and the volunteer put the young man wise to this. Two days later a smiling and relieved 'client' assured him that it was now quite all right. In other words, an uncomplicated exchange of information between two young men probably prevented an unwanted pregnancy and, equally important, may well have prevented an incipient psycho-sexual problem. Had the need been for help with a relationship problem, whether hetero- or homosexual, or with an unwanted pregnancy, the request would normally be passed on to an officer or counsellor.

Here again, however, a balance has to be struck between being available if wanted, yet not prying or probing for problems. Fortunately, the volunteers who have worked with the project so far have been alive to this and accept that in the long term the best approach is the 'soft sell'; that is, Grapevine workers make themselves known for what they are, they do not pester, and they are prepared to go at the pace demanded—and to be used or not—by the group among whom they are working. This is a mature approach, which demands patience and understanding of a high order.

Individuality of approach is another factor on which the workshop training places considerable emphasis. Volunteers have opportunities for trying out on each other, in role play, the various ways in which contact with strangers can be made, but there is no single approved way and everyone is encouraged to find out for himself what comes naturally and feels most comfortable and to observe how others get through the shyness barrier. The fact that Grapevine workers are so obviously themselves, devoid of technique, has undoubtedly helped them to win acceptance as the genuine article. Brian Ashley says about training objectives:[3]

> There is a danger that the use of the term 'training' in itself
> may imply a capacity to produce a ready-made product who
> can 'fit' into a tailor-made situation. The foregoing should
> indicate that this is impossible and, in any case, undesirable.
> Professional people must be allowed the capacity to respond
> to situations, to contribute to the development of those
> situations and not be merely expected to respond mechanic-
> ally according to some stereotyped view of their role.

This has been a training objective of Grapevine from the start, thanks to the wise advice we received in the early planning stages and to a realistic appreciation of the work situation which is totally unstructured and in which all manner of demands may be made on the volunteers. There can be no substitute for good sense and confidence in themselves and their colleagues.

Summary

It is premature to draw conclusions now, when the project has just entered its second year and has only had ten months in the Centre. As previously mentioned, a full report will be produced on the two-year period July 1972–June 1974. Hard data are being collected by the volunteers on every contact made, and these are being divided into those contacts where a need is expressed, and those where it is not. Further analysis of needs and outcomes can be correlated with estimated age and status, contact point and whether this was the first, second, third or subsequent contact. A further broad classification is in terms of 'white', 'black', 'brown' and 'other'. In the first seven months, 535 contacts were made outside the Centre and it is expected that this will reach several thousand in the second year. As each batch of contact sheets is processed, the data will be looked at from the point of view of trends which require further study in depth.

A feature of the project which arouses interest is undoubtedly the care with which support has been built in, at all levels. Support for the volunteers has already been described. The field officers, counsellors and project manager also have weekly support meetings, some of which are used for case presentation led by a young psychiatrist introduced to the project by the External Supervising Consultant; in addition, the latter leads a group discussion every three weeks when wider issues are also examined.

It is interesting that the effort involved in expanding the Grapevine group as fast as possible in the first year put internal communications under some strain, and a major part of the solution has been to redouble the emphasis on regular attendance at support meetings, both by volunteers and by field staff and counsellors. Finally, the project has benefited greatly from the manner in which the main sponsoring body, the Family Planning Association, has allowed Grapevine to work out its own strategy with the help of those advisors it chooses to call in as the need arises. This type of support is crucial for experimental work, but not every project is so fortunate.

Support has also been forthcoming from workers in the two boroughs of Islington and Camden in which the project is working. Liaison with professional colleagues in the community is an important part of the function of the two field officers, and it is greatly to their personal credit that such a sound basis for mutual

pport and collaboration has already been achieved in Islington and
ıs begun so encouragingly in Camden.

An object of this article has been to stir interest, but not to
ıggest that answers have yet been found to every question. In our
nal year, there is a great deal to be done before we ourselves are
.tisfied that we have done full justice to the Grapevine idea. That
ıe basic idea is on the right lines, we have no doubts at all.

otes

Mary Morse, *The Unattached,* Penguin, 1965.
'Facts about teenagers (England and Wales)', issued by the Press and
Information Department, Family Planning Association, Margaret Pyke
House, 27-35 Mortimer Street, London W1A 4QW, June 1972:

1 An estimated 3,996 girls under 16 became pregnant in 1971.
2 An estimated 1,350 girls under 16 gave birth in 1971.
3 There were approximately 20,000 illegitimate births to girls aged
   16-19 in 1971.
4 Abortions to girls under 16 in 1971 numbered 2,646, whereas in 1970
   there were only 1,791. (Registrar General)
5 Abortions to girls under 20 numbered 21,879 in 1971, in 1970 there
   were 15,020. (Registrar General)
6 One in three teenage brides is pregnant.
7 Approximately seven in ten teenage births are illegitimate or conceived
   before marriage.
Scotland
8 In 1970 there were 110 births to girls under 16.
9 In 1970 there were 2,450 illegitimate births to girls between 16-20.
10 One in four teenage brides is pregnant.
11 Two in three teenage births are illegitimate or conceived before
   marriage.
12 Teenage abortions totalled 929 in 1971.
Venereal disease (figures from Government Chief Medical Officer)
1 In 1970 9,210 teenagers were suffering from gonorrhoea whilst in
   1969 there were 7,278.
2 In 1970 475 of those suffering from gonorrhoea were under 16, in
   1969 there were 403.
Brian Ashley, 'Professional Training Objectives', *Scottish Journal of Youth
and Community Work* 1 (2), summer 1973, pp. 38-40.

9 The community worker as stranger: the effects of housing design

David N. Thomas

Community workers do not always appreciate the extent to which they are strangers to the community they wish to serve. Many workers may have a strong sense of identification with the needs and problems of the inhabitants of an area but may be unaware that their feelings of attachment or belongingness are not reciprocated; the worker may not realise that his identification and commitment do little to mediate between his status as an outsider and the historical and continuing deprivation (and distrust of professionals) of the neighbourhood. It is natural for the worker to assume that there is in the community an understanding and appreciation of his work that will easily overcome suspicion about his motivations to help. The very closeness of relationships that often develop between a community worker and a neighbourhood group can lead even the experienced worker to fudge over the marginality of his position with local people, which exists even when he is well known to the members of a group, and even after he has been tested and 'accepted'. How much more marginal is the position of the worker at the time he attempts to initiate contact with local residents!

The community worker's status as a stranger intervening in the life of a block of flats or a street is not entirely different from that of any newcomer to a community. In the first week of their work, the milkman, postman and caretaker are also strangers to the tenants of an estate; these men are strangers, too, to new families on the estate. Yet the community worker is a stranger in ways which they are not the milkman and those in other peripatetic commercial services are identified both by their class position and their function. The new postman may have a strange face, but his function is known and accepted by the tenants. The community worker, however, is distinguished both by his class position and by the fact that his function is not understood by the tenants. Even a new caseworker may be more easily identified than the community worker by knowledge among tenants of the common characteristics of the families seen to be visited; or (less likely nowadays) by conformity with a well-known stereotype (for instance, the large-hatted lady stepping out of a Morris Minor).

People and systems develop a variety of encounter mechanisms through which strangers are recognised and their activities questioned. The effects of planning and design of neighbourhood housing on expanding and contracting the opportunities for such encounters have been documented notably by Jane Jacobs and Oscar Newman. This paper explores a fundamental proposition in the works of Jacobs and Newman: that the availability of opportunities for informal social interaction will help to determine people's capacity and inclination to think and act collectively in respect to community issues. Jacobs, for instance, writes: 'Formal public organisations in cities require an informal life underlying them, mediating between them and the privacy of the people in the city'.[1] Likewise, Newman argues that the manipulation of building and spatial configurations can release potential behavioural attitudes and positive social relationships.[2] He gives many examples of design types and design alterations to streets and housing projects which have resulted in an increased social interaction between tenants and a greater inclination towards activity in joint collective enterprises.

We have already indicated that the community worker is to be placed within the category of stranger as he sets about his task of 'getting the feel' of an estate. In the next section we shall consider aspects of his intervention that seem to be affected by some of the physical characteristics of housing estates. Of course, many factors may affect the outcome of a worker's intervention. For example, the worker may have adopted the 'wrong' approach or chosen an unrepresentative nucleus to form a tenants' group; or he may have chosen to run with an issue that is of no interest or priority to the majority of tenants. This paper examines a factor that is rarely considered by community workers as affecting the outcome of their work—the way in which a particular design or combination of architectural solutions influences the degree of social integration of tenants on an estate and, hence, the worker's opportunity for interaction and subsequent organisation.

The 'open' and 'closed' estate

We begin by defining two types of flatted housing estates. The first type comprises those built between and after the wars, consisting of several stories, usually not more than six or seven. The flats on the stories above ground level are reached by one or several open staircases, and the flats themselves open out onto a balcony which often runs from one end of the building to the other. The ground floor flats open directly onto a common internal courtyard, usually referred to as 'the square' or 'the yard'. The flats will be grouped either on all sides of the square, or on only three; the essential point is that all flats overlook the square (in which car spaces and pram sheds are often located) and it is usually possible to see from any flat all the doors and windows of flats on the other sides of the square. We call this type of accommodation a *socially open* estate.

The second kind of estate consists of buildings several stories high, broken up into several staircases. The entrances of these staircases open on to the grounds of the estates, and flats are located at each floor around the staircase. The flats open out to a small lobby on each floor. Only a proportion of flats have windows that look out over the common interior square; it is possible to see only the windows of other tenants in the square but not their front doors. A tenant standing at his front door can survey only the doors of those small number of flats (usually between two and four) on his particular landing. We call this type of development a *socially closed* estate. We would also describe as socially closed those more modern estates of superblocks served by a bank of two to four lifts, where a typical floor has a central corridor with flats lining both sides.

On an open estate the milkman and postman can be seen on their rounds; on a closed estate a housewife has no means of knowing where the milkman is; whether he has finished his rounds or forgotten her staircase and landing. Some kinds of strangers visiting an estate will prefer the closed kind: the criminal, policeman or young man courting a girl can enter a staircase from the yard and, even if he were observed, there would be no way of knowing which of the flats he was visiting. Criminals who live on a closed estate have little to fear from informers active on open estates, of which there are many kinds. For example, the *Guardian* of 20 September 1973 reports how tenants discovered and chased off a fraud investigator from the Department of Health and Social Security. 'Residents', said the report, 'were suspicious of a man who sat in a red Ford Escort outside their flats for long periods on several days. After a week, one of the tenants asked the driver what his business was . . . "The man was getting on everybody's nerves." '

For another instance, the demonstrations organised by the tenants' association at Chaucer House in the London borough of Southwark, which excluded housing and social service officers from their rooms on the estate, were successful partly because the tenants had surveillance of the square and three entrances. They were immediately able to detect the presence of a stranger within or approaching the square. The open nature of Chaucer House also allowed members of the tenants' association to intervene when families were threatened with eviction or when children from outside were observed breaking into empty flats. The two key characteristics of these open estates are, first, that tenants can efficiently monitor, scrutinise and question the presence and activities of strangers on the estate. The design provides many surveillance opportunities of other flats and of parts of the estate (e.g. squares, balconies) that tenants come to regard as being private or semi-private territory. On closed estates, effective monitoring of strangers is precluded by design; there are few surveillance opportunities and little, if any, sense of control over public parts of the estate. The second characteristic is that an open estate facilitates social interaction between tenants, particularly on the level of their own stories around the block. On a closed estate, a tenant is unlikely to be on more than nodding terms with people on his own staircase and rarely does he know a family on another staircase, though he may be familiar with one or two of the families on his own landing. This isolation of people within their own flats is as striking within corridors of superblocks. These characteristics of open and closed estates are important because the community worker is initially a stranger and, in the nature of his work, concerned with creating an action system for change (e.g. a tenants' committee or an old people's club) which will partly depend for its initiation and growth on the scope and intensity of social relationships on the estate.

The estate design that criminals prefer is unsympathetic to the activities of community workers; the nature of open estates deters the criminal but can facilitate the intervention and organisation tactics of community workers. The stranger who enters an estate as a criminal wishes to preserve his anonymity and has a vested interest in perpetuating a socially fragmented community. The stranger who comes as a community worker wishes to shed his anonymity and has a vested interest in consolidating the social integration of the tenants and their sense of collective identity and responsibility.

Initiating work on an open estate

Intervention in an open estate is a testing and demanding experience for the community worker. He may be conscious that his activity of 'hanging around' in the square talking to people is attracting the curiosity and attention of tenants; and the tenants themselves (or, more likely, the caretakers or porters) will show an aggressive interest in the reasons for his presence. He attracts attention because his behaviour is ambiguous and similar to that of strangers who traditionally are not welcome in estate life, such as the fraud investigator or the plain-clothes policeman. Newman has shown that there is a limit to the degree of ambiguous behaviour tolerated in a zone that residents regard as private or semi-private; whilst it is rare for people to question the presence of individuals on a street pavement, he says, 'individuals within a territorially restricted zone are required to efficiently pursue a goal or purpose; lingering becomes a privilege available to recognized residents following prescribed rituals'.[3] The community worker neither is a recognised resident nor does he follow prescribed rituals; his behaviour is ambiguous in the extreme. During the stage of hanging about on an estate, watchful residents might consider him to be a potential fraud investigator, plain-clothes policeman, housebreaker, debt-collector, child molester, car thief, missionary from an evangelical sect or political agitator. A female community worker might be seen as a potential prostitute. A community worker who is aware that his activities are open to misinterpretation may feel extremely anxious at this phase of his intervention and wish for the greater anonymity provided by closed estates.

The physical expansiveness of an open estate may provoke a strong sense of engagement on the part of the worker and promote a high level of expectation on the part of residents. Because of this, the worker may find it difficult to keep his options open and distinguish his intervention as an 'information-gathering process'. On an open estate the process of contact-making and information-seeking is an *inclusive intervention*: the ease with which the worker is observed and the more efficient exchange of information within the informal public life of an open estate involves more tenants than those with whom he talks directly. Conversely, these initial interventions on a closed estate are *exclusive*, to the degree that the interaction between the worker and the tenant takes place within the relatively unobserved territory of the staircase landing. This notion of inclusive and exclusive activity is best conceived of as a continuum; there may be some closed estates that are closer to the inclusive end of the continuum because of the length of tenure and homogeneity of the population; and some open estates nearer the exclusive end on account of size and turnover of tenants. On the whole, however, open estates tend to be more inclusive and closed estates tend to be more exclusive.

Because the worker's intervention on open estates is perceived as inclusive activity, many of the observing tenants may expect to be visited by the worker. It is not clear how this will redound to the concerns of the worker. It is likely that although some tenants may be aware, through estate gossip, of the worker's activity, they may not have grasped the precise or even general nature of his interest and work. He may find that some doors are slammed in his face while other tenants are eager to talk with him. But whatever the outcome, an inclusive intervention may give tenants a marginally more autonomous position *vis à vis* a worker. To be forewarned means to be forearmed, and tenants can make some decision, before a possible encounter, about how they will respond to this particular stranger, should he knock on their door. The worker may also find that when the design of the building makes an inclusive intervention possible, he is better able to make contact with tenants who refuse to see him or who are reluctant to open their doors to unknown callers. The same diffidence to interact with strangers is especially difficult to overcome on the relatively unobserved parts of closed estates like staircases, public grounds, lifts and enclosed corridors.

Inclusive intervention may affect the community worker's objectives in other ways. For instance, tenants might seek him out because they are interested in those issues which they understand the worker to have discussed with tenants already visited. On the other side, inclusive intervention may lead to the worker being 'warned off' the estate. This could happen if a tenant or caretaker who has taken money from prospective tenants in exchange for recommending them for a vacant flat hears about the presence of the worker and, rightly or wrongly, fears that his key-money may be jeopardised. It is also common for a caretaker or a long-established resident who feels paternalistic towards the other tenants to warn off the worker, if he is suspicious of his activities. Another kind of warning-off takes place, for instance, when the worker hears that there is another community work agency already active on the estate or that an extant tenants' group is 'non-political' and will not respond helpfully to the worker's efforts to organise opposition to a rent rise. These different kinds of 'warnings-off' are more likely to occur (and it is well that they occur as soon as possible, so that the worker can modify his approach accordingly) where intervention is inclusive.

An estate of the open kind may provide more opportunity for the worker to consolidate the contacts he has made in the initial stages of his intervention. He can, for example, make a casual appearance in the square where there is a good deal of observed community activity. Here he can talk with men mending their cars, come into contact with women crossing the yard to and from the shops or join in a game of football with the estate's teenagers. This consolidation of early contacts is, like the making of those contacts, an inclusive activity on the estate in as much as he is observed by tenants on other parts of the estate who may be walking along, hanging out washing on balconies or gossiping on their doorsteps. This kind of estate offers the worker opportunities for participation in the social life of the square as well as the bonus of having this participation observed by other tenants. Square activities present a variety of pretexts or niches for the worker to be seen edging into the informal social life of the estate. These pretexts also offer him occasions to make manifest other aspects of himself and to know better the people with whom he will be working. Opportunities also arise, obviously in a setting such as a public house; for instance, a social services department worker wrote:

> I see our 'surgery' as an advice point and as a way of giving a broader perspective of myself to the community and for me to acquire a broader perspective of the local community and the people I work with in other roles. I feel it is very important that social workers let themselves be seen in roles other than casework roles; that is, I no longer see the value of a social worker being seen as a mysterious lady who steps out of a Morris Minor and disappears up the stairs. This means that social workers have to find pretexts in order to let themselves be seen quite differently in the neighbourhood in which they work and the advice session and the time I put in in the pub afterwards, has given me such a valuable pretext. Other

pretexts seem to be found in shopping in the area and in the contact with schools and play groups. I think there is a need for the social worker to prove himself in a community setting and thereby make his service more relevant. This might be better than the current fashion for enticing the community to make better use of the area office. The social worker must go out into his patch and find a little niche somewhere and these niches can be found in the most funny ways. For instance, one of the pretexts I used was to establish myself as a reasonable darts player in the local pub. Of course, finding niches of this kind might be easier for a man, though I suppose female social workers could find a pretext in places like mothers' groups and dress-making classes etc. A general point behind this is that agencies and the social services acquire credibility only through the efforts of their workers.

Intervention on a closed estate

What does all this mean to the worker intervening on a closed estate? If there are few opportunities for inclusive intervention, the worker may have to look for various areas outside estate life where tenants are to be found in informal social interaction. (Of course, this search for an extra-mural source of intervention might also be helpful in an open-estate situation.) Some of the most common areas of extra-mural interaction include local public houses, play groups, schools, launderettes, corner shops and, in some circumstances, the church. Each of these situations can sustain informal social contact among tenants which the community worker may want to exploit to facilitate his intervention in the life of the estate. The ability of each of these situations to sustain such contact among residents will depend on a number of local factors. In the case of the school, for instance, interaction between parents will depend largely on the policy of the head and the staff in encouraging or inhibiting parents' participation in the life of the school. Or it may depend, as will the outcome of a school's drive to involve parents, on whether there is a substantial proportion of working mothers on the estate who are unable to deliver or collect their children from school.

Another method of facilitating intervention open to the worker on a closed estate is that of 'sponsorship'; that is, the worker might find a well-known personality or authority figure living on or near the estate whose support for his interests will generate a positive response to him from most of the tenants. Possibilities for sponsors include a respected shopkeeper, caretaker, social worker, teacher, councillor, priest or indigenous leader. For example, here is an account of a worker wishing to intervene to help residents of a small terrace isolated on the fringe of a huge closed estate. The worker records:

> The vicar suggested that I might like to go to some of the local pubs to meet some of the people that he knows. We went to the Rose and Standard, and then to the Hand in Hand and talked with various people the vicar obviously knows well. We met Pat who was waving a letter which he had had from the borough which he said was equivalent to a referencing letter and wanted to know what could be done about it and whether or not people had any say as to where they were moved to. The vicar explained that I was here to deal with the people in the area and that this would be just the sort of thing that I might be able to take up with them, and I made an arrangement to meet Pat for lunch the next day to see the various letters that he had had and to talk to him about what might be done about it. We went to the A B C, which is mainly a pub for young people, where again the vicar is very well known. I was extremely impressed with this local contact which he had made during his short time as vicar in the area and he was very willing to take me around some more if I wished.

Sponsorship of this kind is extremely problematical. In the first place, a worker may not want to be seen in alliance with an authority figure like the caretaker or councillor if, for instance, he suspects a hostile attitude on the part of tenants to the housing management or where he hopes to work with tenants to effect changes in their housing situation. He may not know at the early stages of intervention whether the sponsorship of a particular individual will facilitate or hinder his work. But he can be certain that no sponsoring figure will command the support and respect of every tenant; a decision, for instance, to work alongside the caretaker may win support from some tenants but may alienate others.

Tactics and design

Building design is also relevant to the selection of stratagems used in community action. Consider, for an example, the use of a tenants' petition. The petition serves many purposes for community groups. Primarily, it strengthens the hand of a community group in its negotiations with the authority about a particular local grievance or quest for improvement in some aspect of estate or neighbourhood life. But, just as important, the petition is an instrument of community education; it enables knowledge of the work of the sponsoring group to be disseminated by the signature-collectors. Residents are assured that someone is doing something about a particular issue. In turn, the petition's sponsors learn of residents' views about the issue and perhaps about other matters affecting their well-being. Additionally, the signature-collecting exercise enables the sponsors to identify and encourage recruits to the work of the group. Media coverage of the petition promotes further awareness of the interests of the group, consolidating people's knowledge of its goals and, by the very act of achieving publicity, enhances the status of the group in the constituent community. These same dynamics operate in other group actions like surveys and questionnaires. Such actions on an open estate are conducted as inclusive activities. Tenants are encouraged to sign if they have observed their neighbours signing. This is especially important if the issue is controversial or sensitive so that a tenant might feel vulnerable or exposed to victimisation. One of the most frequent questions of petitioners on housing estates is: 'Who else has signed; how many signatures have you got already?' On a closed estate, however, petitioning is a lonely exercise; not only are people reluctant to open doors on their landings but they have little sense that they are engaging in a community activity. Signing seems an individual act of defiance. Of course, the intensity of feeling will vary with the issue and the standing of the community group.

Brager and Specht point out that the sequence and timing of a community worker's efforts are 'influenced by the extent to which constituents have previously shared group experiences . . . only rarely do workers recruit members who have not had prior involvement with one another . . . the timing [of a group's development] is influenced by the particular values and prior experience of the actors, as well as by the exigencies of the social climate and the ways in which the external environment infringes on their efforts.'[4] An important part of this environment is the design of the estate and the worker must consider this factor when choosing among his methods of intervention. For instance, the public meeting

called by the worker or by an embryonic group is often a hazardou
form of initial intervention for the worker. Residents are asked to
give a public commitment of their interests in and concerns about a
particular issue; they may feel diffident, or worried about appearing
foolish by being the only ones to turn up; they may feel encouraged
by knowing what other residents think about the issue in question
Calling people to come to a public meeting as an initial way of
organising them depends for its success on the quality of the
informal social life among tenants. The worker must search for
opportunities for tenants informally to test out each others
reactions to the meeting and to gain confidence from one another's
interest and commitment to attend. Other factors—the size of the
estate, length of tenure and stability of the population and its
homogeneity in terms of family size, composition, race, class and
age—will be pertinent. The worker may have nothing more than an
impression of these factors at the early stages of his intervention. But
the assumption on the part of a worker who encourages an
embryonic group to call a public meeting is that there is an
inclination among the tenants of the estate to think and act
collectively. He must test out this assumption before committing
himself or a group to the public meeting as a way of organising
tenants. One important test is that of estimating the degree of
informal involvement among tenants that can be observed within the
estate and which the building design permits.

The degree of such involvement will affect the ways in which
tenants will work together. Clearly it will matter whether the
committee members already know one another or if the committee
meeting is the first opportunity they have had to interact with one
another. It must be borne in mind that a great deal of the work of
committees takes place outside the actual meetings. Planning and
the evaluation of a meeting, for instance, often occurs in the pub.
Officers make decisions on a daily basis about important matters. If
members of a committee, particularly in its early stages of
development, do not plan for such work as meeting other members
or keeping fellow officers informed of developments and decisions,
effective communication and co-operation within the committee
must grow out of chance informal encounters between members. It
is our suggestion that these are more likely on an open estate than on
a closed estate. Furthermore, recruitment to a committee is easier
where opportunities for chance encounters are present; so is
dissemination of the achievements and plans of the tenants'

ssociation which, on a closed estate, may depend solely on more
ormalised means of information—news-sheets or leaflets.

Conclusion

ntervention must be planned for. An important aspect of this
planning is that the intervention be *seen*. The design features of open
estates allow a worker's intervention to be inclusive. In addition,
they are often found to provide a varied number of opportunities for
informal social interaction among tenants which can facilitate group
formation and development. Our purpose in this paper has been to
demonstrate how the dynamic interaction between design and
intervention are related to these aspects of community work.

References

1   Jane Jacobs, *The Death and Life of Great American Cities*, Penguin, 1972,
    p. 68.
2   Oscar Newman, *Defensible Space*, Architectural Press, 1972, p. 206.
3   Newman, op. cit., p. 65.
4   G. Brager and H. Specht, *Community Organising*, Columbia University Press,
    1973, pp. 82–3.

10 **Settlements as agencies for social change**

Graham Richies

Early Settlements

Settlements, those late Victorian bases of social philanthropy and reform, have recently engaged themselves in a process of reinterpreting their roles in the 1970s. Many would say this task was long overdue. However, there is no doubt that the early founders so located their Settlements and endowed them with such multi-purpose constitutions that those who now wish to engage in community work from inner city bases have only to seize the potential which Settlements still offer. Ninety years after the first, Toynbee Hall, was founded, there are still tasks to be performed.

Settlements are to be found in the inner urban areas of most of the large cities. The majority are in London, but they have also been set up in Bristol, Birmingham, Edinburgh, Dundee, Glasgow, Liverpool and Manchester. Only a very few have been forced to move because of urban redevelopment programmes and the very fact that they are still active in the inner city is one small indicator of the slow pace of social reform. In some ways, Settlements today could be described as gaunt monuments to an emasculated Victorian philanthropy, but it should be pointed out that the physical structures and size of most of their buildings suggest that the plant, if not the ethos, is here to stay. The question is whether such institutions have a legitimate role today.

The constitutions of most Settlements concern themselves with the health and welfare of the poorer classes and the relief of poverty. These are phrases from the past, tinged perhaps by patronising sentiments, but, as expressions of the reality of most modern community action, they are peculiarly apt. The men and women from the universities, different religious denominations, from colleges and schools who were involved in the pioneering work of the early Settlement movement certainly thought in terms of caring and providing much needed services. Some of them also engaged in research and investigation and, in the context of social reform, were responsible for influencing the social and educational policies of their local authorities. The law and medicine were also recipients of the attention of early Settlement workers. Certainly, Settlements were, and in some cases still are, unthinking bastions of middle-class values, seeking to befriend, guide and lead. But having said that, they also had the potential to encourage and influence reform. Their strength lay in the fact that they were voluntary agencies well endowed in ideas and finance; they were independent in their actions and multi-purpose in conception, if not always in operation. While they were neighbourhood based, work and influence could extend well beyond the immediate locality. It would also seem that at the time when they were active in the field of social reform, they prompted research and a spirit of radical enquiry.

Losing the way

Why did Settlements lose their way? This aspect of the Settlements' history has not been adequately researched, but it would appear that the development of the welfare state was certainly a crucial factor. As educational, health and social services became increasingly the responsibility of the state, the Settlements found it difficult to make adequate provision from slender resources. Voluntary agencies themselves either regrouped into larger, single-purpose institutions or, like the Settlements, became lost. Not many Settlements went to the wall, but they had to struggle to survive. A further cause for their demise possibly lay in the fact that universities and, in particular, Departments of Extra-Mural Studies and Institutes of Adult Education were much more effective in providing for the educational needs of adults.

At the same time, one could claim that Settlements lost their way because they came to represent, along with the authorities and the majority of voluntary agencies, a philosophical and physical expression of a 'consensus' approach to social welfare; they became identified with 'welfare' (perhaps they always had been) and voluntary effort; they continued to provide services when other better equipped organisations existed to provide those very services;

they emphasised services, treated symptoms and forgot the cause
and the huge potential of their investigatory and reforming roles.

There was, and perhaps still is, a tendency for the patrons o
Settlements to believe that they know what is best for the workin
class. Such people find it difficult to understand that the ver
existence of a Settlement demonstrates the actuality of Disraeli'
and Marx's 'two Nations'. In other words, Settlements remained par
of the problem without becoming aware of the inheren
contradictions of their situation in a society whose values and more
were changing. Settlements are not the only voluntary agencies i
this position, but it is important that Settlements as well as othe
community work agencies are aware that, in seeking to promot
specific changes in society, they are themselves agents o
considerable social control—if they so choose.

Revival

During the late sixties there were the beginnings of a revival in the
Settlement idea and Settlement work, which is now taking shape
and, given a strong lead from the newly active British Association of
Settlements, the present developments in Settlement work will
continue. What are the factors that have led to these developments?
It is too soon to assess the different influences correctly, but they
would seem to stem from a reaction to the practice of Settlement
work over the last fifty years.

The development of community work in this country during the
sixties has certainly had its effect, along with the radical
campaigning of large voluntary agencies such as CPAG, Shelter and
the squatting movement. Settlements have been forced to consider
the views, feelings and needs of local, working-class people (in other
words their clients) in the reformulation of their policies and
programmes, if only to keep going. Some now employ community
workers (e.g. Blackfriars, Cambridge House, The Albany,
Manchester University Settlement), and this fact alone has
prompted active discussion within individual Settlements and BAS
as to the question of local participation in Settlement affairs. At the
same time, this development has begun to attract a new type of
person to enter Settlement work, both in the key positions of
Warden or Director, and in the project work which many
Settlements are now promoting.

Clearly, staff members have very personal reasons for wishing to work in Settlements, but there seems to be one common factor: they wish to work in agencies in which they feel they can express and develop their own ideas. Many of them one might describe as refugees from authority and bureaucracy—from the school system, social service departments, the law and the church. Settlements are being increasingly regarded as agencies which provide the opportunities to develop alternative approaches to some of today's problems. Legal and financial problems are being tackled through Money Advice Centres and welfare rights projects; new job opportunities are being explored through new careers programmes; community arts schemes are bringing live drama into the neighbourhood; experiments are being carried out in residential living; national attention is being focused on the needs of illiterate people.

It is precisely because of their independence, multi-purpose philosophy and their inner city action bases that they are attractive to people with ideas and abilities. Writing from the position of a Director of a Settlement, one can only say that there are few jobs in which young people today have the freedom to develop their own thinking and express this in action. In that Settlements can now attract personnel with knowledge, experience and training in all the current fields of community action and reform, then clearly the impact upon the Settlements themselves will be great.

A further reason for the current revival is the increasing recognition of the opportunities for change (though perhaps reform is a more appropriate word) which Settlements offer. These opportunities have always been present, but for very long periods have not been seized upon. To the social action worker, the action-researcher, the social worker who wishes to work with people in new forms of individual and group care, Settlements present ready-made bases for urban action. They are situated in the most depressed areas of the cities; they can (not all do) offer flexibility of action and a residential base; they encourage ideas; they can house a number of exciting and interlocking projects because of their physical size; they have money (though some are not prepared to use it); more importantly they have links through their Councils (governing bodies) and through their grass-roots location with people who can bring about change. This last factor is important, for the links with the establishment can often help to cut through red tape and bureaucracies, while the political potential of participants

in action programmes is enormous. This is not to suggest that all
Settlements would accept this view of the position of their organi
sations, it is merely to state the potential which they command.

The decisive factor in the re-emergence of Settlements has been
the development programmes of the British Association of
Settlements. Geoffrey Clarkson, until recently the BAS Devel
opment Officer,[1] described them thus in the Annual Report of the
Association for 1972–3:

> Between 1965 and 1968, David Collet, then Warden of
> Blackfriars Settlement, initiated the Blackfriars Federation.
> This was an experiment to test whether a group of
> Settlement could benefit by pooling experience and sharing
> a central resource person. The high points of this project
> were the beginning of the transformation of the Lady
> Florence Institute, Deptford, now known as 'The Albany',
> continuing developments at the Blackfriars Settlement and
> the conviction that this project could be regarded as a pilot
> scheme for a national programme for BAS.

In 1968 the Gulbenkian Foundation, which had financed the
Blackfriars Federation, agreed to support the proposals for a
three-year BAS Development Programme, but it was not until
1971–2 that the BAS established its aims and objectives, set its work
programme and three-year budget, and obtained the necessary
financial resources. In February 1973 the BAS adopted the
following statement of common purpose:

> The purpose of a Settlement is to encourage and enable
> people to move towards the vision of a caring, sharing
> society; to bring about the maximum involvement of the
> group, neighbourhood or community in solving the
> problems that concern them, in participating in the decision
> that affect them and in running their own affairs.

> To this end we are concerned actively to promote:
> 1 Interdependence and the principle of mutual aid.
> 2 A practical approach to problems and solutions but with
>   an awareness of how each decision relates to wider
>   theories of social change.
> 3 The adoption of realistic goals and reasonable
>   compromise without subordinating our values to those of
>   funding agencies and 'authorities'.

4 Social experiment and the need to report and act on the result of that experiment.
5 An insistence on creating and increasing rights and responsibilities rather than privileges.
   We are determined to avoid:
1 Concentrating on symptoms to the exclusion of causes.
2 Focusing on a locality while ignoring wider needs and issues.
3 The assumption of prerogatives—elitist, paternalist, professional—i.e. behaviour which tends to create or perpetuate unequal relationships.
4 Dishonest manipulation.

The aims of the Association have now been expressed as:

1 To provide the necessary support services enabling the Settlements to work towards their common purpose.
2 To ensure that the work of Settlements is reflected in social reform.

Phase II (1973–6) of the B A S Development Programme is funded by the Home Office and through substantially increased affiliation fees from the twenty-four member Settlements. However, it is the two aspects of the Programme which merit some attention, because there may well be messages for other agencies.

The BAS Programme

The services provided by B A S are essentially concerned with helping Settlements to redefine their purposes, develop open and flexible organisational structures, provide expertise and support for management problems (which by implication includes questions of participation) and ensure that sufficient finances are raised and effectively used. These are all exceedingly difficult areas not only because of the subject-matter, but because each Settlement is constitutionally independent and autonomous. Yet, it must be said that all Settlements, despite the different emphasis which they put on their work (some are more inclined to social action, others to individual care, others to providing community services), need the services outlined above, because these areas all present similar problems. Often the most difficult task is to help a Settlement (and other agencies for that matter) to work out its purpose and its programme before it concerns itself with finance. The reason for this is because finance often becomes the sole *raison d'être* for deciding whether or not the agency can develop a programme; voluntary agencies thus feel they cannot operate unless they can first obtain grant-aid from a statutory source. In this way a vicious circle of financial impotence leading to poverty of ideas is set up.

The second aspect of the Programme is based upon the twin assumptions that the work of Settlements in certain fields is of such social or educational importance that the issues must be raised in a national context, and the corollary, that B A S itself, which is no more than a joint collective of all its members, should sponsor Conferences and initiate campaigns based upon agreed priorities. The National Literacy Conference held in November 1973 was the first practical result of this policy and the National Literacy Campaign is now under way. The intent of this campaign is not to encourage Settlements or voluntary agencies up and down the country to develop schemes for adult illiterates, but to ensure that the Department of Education and Science and the Local Education Authorities provide sufficient resources, and in the right way, to deal with the problem.

The role of Settlements today

Given that society's problems are as acute and probably more complex than ever, and the continued physical presence of Settlements, how should they view their roles? This is a difficult question to answer as each Settlement will no doubt wish to adopt its own stance. However, there seem to be three choices open to Settlements: they can close down or be bought up, as some have done; they can continue as before, or can face up again to a society still divided by class, wealth and opportunity and reinterpret their original purposes today. These purposes are: to act as independent, multi-purpose agencies not tied to any one particular ideology, system of institutionalised care or academic/training disciplines; to ask penetrating questions; to help to provide the necessary analysis of problems and demonstrate through their work alternative approaches to problems which their locations force upon them. This may include looking at Settlements themselves as part of the established order of charity. They should also seek locally and nationally to bring about the changes they think are desirable and necessary.

In their alliance with community work and, increasingly one hopes, with social action, Settlements should be one of the group of agencies and individuals who are questioning the operation of the welfare state and the growing institutionalisation and professionalisation of human care in our society. For the Settlements this is a difficult but necessary task, as they were among those early pioneers of modern welfare services. This is not to decry the need for people to care for each other in society, but is to suggest that one must not forget the need for structural changes in our society, and the value of encouraging alternative approaches. The alternative approaches, of marginal importance today, may be of crucial importance tomorrow.

For detailed information of the work of Settlements, contact British Association of Settlements, 7 Exton Street, London SE1 8UE (Tel. 01-261-1919).

Note

1   Bill Taylor is now B A S Development Officer.

Part IV   Research

11 Research and community work

Ray Lees

It is the purpose of this paper to suggest a new framework for developing a dynamic relationship between the activities of community work and social research. Of course, some use of research is already an integral part of community work practice. Every professional worker needs to assemble adequate and reliable data about those with whom he works, and about their background and environment. The community worker is concerned with something more than individual cases. He needs to assemble reliable data about a 'community', in whatever way this rather ambiguous term is defined.[1] Because the community worker is concerned with understanding and working in a complex social situation, it therefore is natural that he should use techniques and information derived from the field of social research. Whether he is collecting information from existing sources of demographic, economic and social data or conducting his own modest neighbourhood survey, he is already taking part in an activity that derives from the tradition of empirical social science.

This affinity between the methods of social science and community work practice has received recognition in professional literature. Goetschius, for example, acknowledges the need for skill in 'helping committees and community groups to identify social welfare needs, design and carry out various kinds of self-survey',[2] the first Gulbenkian study group report on training concludes that the community worker 'has to be able to understand, assess and utilise a variety of research findings and to undertake certain forms of investigation himself',[3] and Leaper devotes a chapter of his book on community work to 'surveying the community'.[4] The same emphasis on the value of research can also be found in more overtly radical writing where the survey approach is seen as a way of increasing neighbourhood awareness in order to promote effective social action.[5] What each of these discussions has in common, is the practice is also greater than is commonly assumed to be the case.

153

tendency to view relevant research techniques as a rather simple activity of ascertaining and recording facts. Research is seen as a way of providing hard information on matters such as sex, age, occupation, income, accommodation, size of family and perhaps attitudes concerning these.

One weakness with this kind of discussion in community work writing is that it often makes so-called 'fact gathering' seem a deceptively easy business. It ignores much of the social science literature on methodology. Some social scientists feel that the dangers of distortion are so great with questionnaire surveys that there are almost no quantitative facts on which one can rely without extensive checking,[6] if at all.[7] When one is administering a questionnaire, the data on the sex of the respondents may be reasonably reliable; but even comparatively simple information on questions such as age, occupation and income have to be elicited with great care; and it is not valid to assume that if the sample is large enough, errors will be eliminated. Reliable estimates of opinion and attitudes are even more difficult to ascertain. Thus the activity of 'fact gathering' is not likely to be easy. Furthermore, any assertions of fact will always be open to challenge and reinterpretation. Even to conduct a modest neighbourhood survey, therefore, a community work practitioner should have some understanding of the basic concepts, methods and limitations of social research.

There is a further disadvantage to the community approach in taking a rather simple and limited view about the nature of social research. To see research simply as a matter of collecting hard facts, is to ignore other perspectives from the social sciences that could prove important to improving community work theory and practice. As well as studying the background and attitudes of people, social research is also concerned with understanding human behaviour and activities. There is a need to know what actually happens in institutions such as schools, social work agencies, planning departments and political parties. If one serious aim of the community approach is to improve political and administrative processes, the community worker should not neglect opportunities to study how these processes actually occur. With the growth of community work itself, it is now important to know what this activity involves and what its impact on a locality is likely to be. Whilst social research is certainly a more complex and hazardous business than it would normally seem from reading community work literature, its potential for interaction with community work

The benefits to be gained from a fuller use of social research in community work practice would not be one-sided. Research in the field of social policy is not simply a question of trying to understand what has already happened. A great deal of the work done in university departments of social administration has the implicit assumption that research findings will help towards promoting social improvement. Much notable work, like the various poverty studies, is clearly geared to this end. Yet there is no certain link between producing evidence of need and ensuring effective political and administrative action to remedy a situation. One of the critical tasks with this kind of research, therefore, remains the effective communication of research findings to the policy-maker and the discovery of ways and means to ensure their absorption into public decision-making. Community work often does seek to influence political decision-making and the implementation of public policies, at least at local level. Seen thus, research in a community work setting may offer the social scientist both the opportunity to study some of the key factors that determine local decision-making and the challenge of trying to influence the outcome in particular situations.

Given that this kind of focus for research is accepted as relevant to community work, questions must follow about who is the best placed and what is the necessary competence to actually carry it out. Given also that there are different types of relevant research activity, it is likely that there should be different answers to these questions in relation to various tasks that can be undertaken. No simple answer can deal with all possible situations. Decisions about research in community work will in practice be limited too by the availability of resources and the acceptability of different types of arrangement to the people involved. The following analysis is based on research experience in a government-sponsored local Community Development Project (CDP), but it also provides a setting for discussing wider considerations.

Community Development Project—an illustration

The Community Development Project programme was initiated in 1969, and has gradually extended its scope to cover twelve local area projects. The programme represents a modest attempt to discover how far the social needs experienced by people in a local community

can be better understood and resolved through closer co-ordination
of all the social welfare agencies, together with the aspirations and
efforts of local people themselves. A fundamental feature of each
local project is the effort to combine action, research and evaluation.
It is assumed that an exploratory approach, using social science
methods of inquiry and evaluation as a built-in support for social
action, constitutes a useful addition to more traditional ways of
tackling problems of social welfare. This is not the place to discuss in
detail the ongoing work of a local project, but rather to draw out
what seems to be some of the operational implications of this
experience for developing an effective relationship between research
and community work.

controversial

Take the question: who should conduct the research? In the CDP,
the procedure has been for an action team to be appointed to the
local authority's staff and a complementary research team formed
from within a university or polytechnic. There is therefore a
specialist and partly independent research team. In official
documents its function has been described as:[8]

(a) collaborating with the project action team in the assess-
    ment of the locality's needs and how they might best be
    met.
(b) monitoring and evaluation of the project and identifying
    its lessons, both as a continuous guide to action during
    the life of the project, and for feeding back to the local
    authority itself and to other local and central interests.

Thus while research and action are employed by different
institutions and probably recruited from different professional
backgrounds, the CDP anticipates an intimate and productive
working relationship between these two teams of people. To
actually achieve this relationship in practice requires, at least in my
experience, considerable overlap between the community work and
research functions.

This overlap soon became apparent in the effort to assess the
locality's need. There were two main approaches to doing this. One
was to establish a set of quantifiable indicators representing as far as
was practicable the significant social characteristics of the area.
Much was drawn together from existing sources such as census data
and the reports of local authority departments, complemented
where necessary with special local studies. The second approach was
to attempt to assess what local people themselves perceived as being

needed for their locality. On the face of it, one would expect to require for this work a team of experts able to gather complete data and present conclusions in a reliable way. The emphasis would be on research skills. But complex material and sophisticated interpretation will not necessarily assist community workers in determining priorities and forms of action. To be meaningful in this context it soon became clear that the focus of social indicators and the expression of felt need would have to be related to the possible community initiatives an action team would be able to support or undertake. Research needed to be integral to the community approach.

In addition, many surveys undertaken in the CDP were initiated with modest research intentions and primarily with the hope of inspiring local people to take some form of collective action. Simply to collect and make known the facts will not guarantee this motivation. One way of trying to gain this was to encourage local groups to join in the process of data collection. It was hoped that their involvement at an early stage would help to sustain interest in subsequently getting something done to improve the situation. With this kind of neighbourhood self-study, sophisticated data-collection skills were given less importance than the goal of stimulating community involvement. The professional contribution called for community work skills as well as knowledge of research techniques.

A similar overlap between action and research occurred with efforts to monitor and evaluate aspects of project work. An important part of any study of community work practice must be the recording and analysis of everyday activities. Such systematic recording is a tedious business for the hard pressed practitioner and could only be assured where there was an interest in research aspects of his work. Where this interest existed, there was the excitement of keeping ongoing records of complex interaction with local people, welfare agencies, local authority decision-making, and other political and administrative processes. But it could not be assumed that what a worker thought had happened or had been the effect of his presence had actually been the case. While individual records might be responsibly and intelligently kept, such an account would remain partial. Further research was needed to interpret situations from other people's viewpoints and to gain a rounded picture of project activities. Only some community workers would understand or be sympathetic to this kind of research activity, which might place in question their own interpretation of events.

Overlap and close collaboration between action and research workers also proved to be necessary if other research strategies were to be operationalised. Comparative and evaluative studies could only be undertaken where practitioners were willing to face the possibility of disclosing failure. Controlled experiments were only feasible if people were prepared to work to a preconceived research design. Immediate benefits from research could only become effective where research workers were able to contribute to project decisions and were also prepared to participate in some action situations. Leaving aside difficult methodological problems about how to measure its effect, it certainly became clear that action-research in a CDP could best take place only where all participants believed this to be worth while and understood its purpose. Given this goodwill and co-operation, the various tasks still required differing degrees of research skill and community work competence.

This need for differing skills can best be illustrated by discussing briefly a specific programme that has emerged as part of the work of the Project. During the initial period of attempting to identify local need, it became clear that the locality had a high level of unemployment; an above average proportion of large families and the elderly in its population; and that low wages were a significant feature in local industry. Each of these factors were indications of low income and suggested that a high proportion of the population would be eligible for welfare benefits of various kinds—social security, health, housing and education. In this situation it was decided to promote a 'welfare rights campaign' to increase the uptake of selective welfare benefits. The campaign was to have the following three elements:

(a) Working with local people, such as tenants' associations, claimants' groups and trade unionists, to increase awareness of welfare rights and to ensure informed local pressure for improving welfare services. The main aim was to promote and support active pressure groups of local people.

(b) Working with the staff of statutory agencies such as social security, social services, health and housing departments. The main aim was to make these organisations more sensitive and responsive to the material needs of their clients.

(c) To promote publicity campaigns on specific welfare benefits and to attempt to monitor their effect. The main aim here was to test various ways of informing the general public of their rights.

The campaign was planned to run over two years and at the time of writing is about halfway through this period. Some of the research has been of a statistical nature concerned with measuring the degree of eligibility and the impact of publicity campaigns, but the relation between a prior research design and subsequent community action has proved to be more tricky. For example, an influential view in the community work field claims that the practitioner should not seek to persuade local people to accept ideas of his own.[9] This 'non-directive approach' makes invidious any attempt to assess community work activities against narrow preconceived objectives. Even when common objectives were accepted, the interaction of interests within a community and changing external circumstances has made modification necessary. A prior research commitment to rigorous procedures in community work is likely to run counter to the need for flexibility and intuition in dealing with practical situations.

The need for flexibility does not negate the role of research into community work initiatives, but it does mean that this kind of research is not simply a matter of controlled experiment and statistical analysis. In order to understand community work activities, the practitioner must himself be interested in research and should be prepared to keep accurate records. Such records will still represent only a partial view. The locally based campaign to promote the uptake of welfare benefits has already made apparent differing community perceptions of its purpose and value. Social security officers, social workers, councillors, local government officials, members of community groups and so on, do not necessarily share a common view. An important role for research in the C D P has been to chart these differing perceptions and to try to identify constraints and obstacles to bringing about improved services.

A new framework

It may be argued that discussion of research in a fairly large scale CDP is not really relevant to community work in other settings. Certainly it is true that not all community projects will have the resources to conduct wide ranging research of this type. In addition, not all workers will be interested in research or consider it relevant to their needs. No doubt what people choose to call 'community work' can also take a wide variety of forms. Nevertheless, if one accepts a recent definition of community work as 'a movement representing on one hand a set of ideals relating to participation by people in their local community and in decisions affecting their daily lives, and on the other hand a concern with deprivation in its social, economic and environmental manifestations',[10] it certainly follows that there is a large area for research activity relevant to this approach. The challenge is to develop the necessary skills to meet this need.

The intention behind the following classification is to provide a focus for developing such skills. By itself, it provides no easy solutions for the research or community worker. Each facet has its own methodological problems and operational difficulties, some of which have already been suggested. However, it is hoped that the following framework will help to provide a way forward in an area where wider discussion is needed for both practical and theoretical reasons.

The order in which the headings are arranged is not intended to suggest descending importance. Each approach should be seen as inter-related.

1 *Survey.* This would be the attempt to gather knowledge about conditions within an area and attitudes towards them. Many quantifiable data can be drawn together from existing sources covering population, housing, health, education and aspects of the economic situation. Special studies might include, for example, the distribution and take-up of social services or the pattern of work and job opportunities. The aim would be to collect data relating to community needs which could be checked and reassessed from time to time. It is also desirable to know what people really feel is needed within a particular locality and how these feelings relate to existing services, including the services of community workers. These attitudes and opinions are also subject to change, and will be particularly difficult to assess. Various research techniques, such as questionnaires and depth interviews, can be used in this work.

2 *Processes.* This would be to describe and analyse what community workers actually do. There is a need to know something of the assumptions of community work practitioners, how they see their working objectives, and how they are able to express these in interaction with individuals and groups. This focus would also study

the impact of community initiatives on official decision-making policy and policy implementation. If one aspiration is to improve these processes, it is important to have on record what procedures are used and in particular the effect of local people's efforts to influence the way things are done.

3 *Action-research.* Research in community work can offer more than a detached once-off assessment of a particular activity. Research findings concerned with quantifiable data, attitudes or processes can, where appropriate, be fed back into the local situation and contribute directly to immediate concerns. Action-research would represent an effort to achieve effective interplay between research and action as part of an ongoing process in a local situation.

4 *Communications.* If research activity is to have influence beyond the local situation, it must be communicated more widely. Community work tends to be caught up in the intricacies and struggles of a local situation. However, lessons derived from such experiences need to be communicated to other professionals and the wider general public. Research in community work should not be obsessively parochial in its concern, but must be prepared to contribute to journals, books and newspapers.

5 *Theory.* Finally, an important aim of community work research should be to test, systematise and expand a body of theoretical knowledge that can help a community worker in his everyday practice. Each local manifestation of need and community work approach to bringing about improvement will not be unique. The extent to which initiatives are capable of being transposed to other settings should be considered in relation to operational techniques, general principles, immediate goals and long-term aims. In doing this, the limitations of the community work approach need to be delineated, as well as its advantages.

Conclusion

This paper has argued that social research can contribute to community work practice in ways not yet commonly explored in practice or in community work literature. To bring this about to any great extent, community workers concerned with research will need to have a broad understanding of methods and perspectives derived from the social sciences. Such insights are necessary for everyday

162   Ray Lees

work in understanding community processes, defining social need and trying to bring about social improvement. Where the resources are available, close co-operation between the practitioner and a research worker can lead to greater precision and more rounded accounts of community initiatives than are possible if seen from only one perspective. Community work is now an expanding field, but if there is to be a comparable increase in knowledge in this area, it will have to come through organised research.

This activity will also require research workers who are prepared to study needs, demands and satisfaction at a local neighbourhood level. Like the community work practitioner, their work will have to be geared to trying to improve a local situation. Social science has yet to be effectively incorporated into the service of local communities. Research in a community work setting does offer one important means for developing this role.

References

1 For a discussion of varying definitions see N. Dennis, 'The popularity of the neighbourhood idea', in R. Pahl (ed.), *Readings in Urban Sociology*, Pergamon, 1968, pp. 74—95.
2 G. W. Goetschius, *Working with Community Groups*, Routledge & Kegan Paul, 1969, p. 165.
3 Gulbenkian Foundation, *Community Work and Social Change*, Longman, 1968, p. 113.
4 R. A. B. Leaper, *Community Work*, National Council for Social Service, rev. ed., 1971, pp 21-40.
5 See, for example 'Housing Improvement Survey' *Community Action* No. 4 1972, pp. 17-25.
6 J. Madge, *The Tools of Social Science*, Longman, 1953.
7 A. V. Cicourel, *Method and Measurement in Sociology*, New York, Free Press, 1964.
8 *Home Office Press Release*, 2 December 1971.
9 T. R. Batten, *The Non-directive Approach to Group and Community Work*, Oxford University Press, 1967.
10 P. Bryers, 'Community Work in 1972' in K. Jones (ed.), *The Year Book of Social Policy in Britain 1972*, Routledge & Kegan Paul, 1973, pp. 212-227.

12 Research and the community

John Greve

Whole libraries of books have been written about how to conduct social research. University departments are devoted to teaching people how to do research, developing research techniques, researching into research. There are growing bodies of specialists of frightening expertise who concentrate on aspects of research like questionnaire design or devising more meticulous and micro-sensitive ways of testing information mathematically once it has been garnered and classified. The expenditure on capital investment and running costs which have gone into computers in the field of social research—often for the slenderest of speculative reasons—runs into millions of pounds in this country alone. It is doubtful whether this expenditure will ever be justified in cost-benefit terms.

Many people are making a living—usually good, not infrequently rich, and on the whole honest—out of social research. I make no comment on market research as conducted by private companies, but it is worth noting that this hybrid of the entertainment and information industries employs some of the most gifted and imaginative people operating in the 'research' field—as well as some of the most tendentious—and uses the most expensive, up-to-date and efficient techniques and hardware. It also pays handsome fees and retainers to more than a few academics who, when they look in another direction, seem to regard action-research in deprived neighbourhoods as corrupting the purity of research, which should never descend into the political equivalent of the market-place.

The growing but still small literature about the functions and techniques of action-research and, more specifically, of the social researcher in the action situation,[1] devote much attention to the difficulties of the research worker. Usually, the preoccupation is with his role as a social scientist contending with ambiguities of role and purpose, changing objectives, nebulous subject matter and the problems of evaluation. These are all proper matters for concern in applied social research—and, indeed, in considering such important topics as the dynamics and techniques of community action, policy formation, or function and change in organisations. It is possible that not enough attention is being paid to these intricate problems. But another role—or potential role—of the social researcher is neglected almost to the point of disdain in this examination of roles and functions. In the community work setting, especially, there is considerable scope for active roles to be played by people trained and experienced in research without compromising their integrity or standards as research workers—though they might have to risk tarnishing their reputations in some quarters.

Government, commerce and industry increasingly employ—or exploit—social research by commissioning studies or utilising the results of work sponsored under other auspices. It is not uncommon for social scientists to be engaged as consultants and, occasionally, seconded on a full-time or part-time basis to government departments. In DHSS, for example, the Chief Scientist has set up a major advisory council and several servicing committees comprised almost equally of doctors and social scientists. The Rothschild 'think tank' represents another comparatively recent initiative by central government to harness the experience and advice of social and other scientists. Other government departments, such as the Central Statistical Office and the Office of Population, Censuses and Surveys, make substantial use of social scientists from outside. Local authorities also call upon their services as consultants or to conduct research. Finally, both central and local government employ academic researchers to study organisation, functioning, efficiency, decision-making procedures (and thus priorities in the allocation of resources) and to make recommendations.

Middle-class residents' groups or pressure groups of different kinds are also assisted by social researchers—some being drawn from their own membership. In relation to the large masses of people living in disadvantaged areas, however, the active involvement of research workers is sporadic and miniscule. The most common form of contact that the poor and deprived have with social researchers is as natives meeting anthropologists. There are some honourable exceptions, but they are still so rare as to be of little more than token significance. The twelve Community Development Projects sponsored by the Home Office, which operate in a variety of settings, provide an opportunity for new co-operative relationships to develop between researchers and residents, as well as between researchers and action teams, but there are strong tendencies in some projects for traditional (observer and anthropological) roles to be maintained, thus stifling much of the potential contribution that researchers could make directly to the community. In some CDP projects action and research teams have maintained an uneasy relationship which can only vitiate any more fruitful input that research workers might otherwise make.

In his chapter (Research and Community Work) Ray Lees has discussed ways of increasing the value of social research to community work by developing a more dynamic relationship between the two. I should like to extend the logic of this approach by suggesting how the skills, experience (which includes accumulated knowledge), and insights of social research can be of more direct value to the community itself, so that the people who are usually the objects of research can become partners and initiators instead.

The central point in my proposal is that for the purposes of community development research workers can, and should, perform functions analagous to those of community workers. In other words, that they should set out to transmit the philosophy and skills of social research to individuals and groups in the community. It is not being proposed that research workers should consequently abandon their more traditional methods and techniques. On the contrary, for without the experience and knowledge gained from rational investigation and testing researchers would not be adequately equipped to move out into other fields and dimensions of research. It will be because they are informed and practised and keep their knowledge and techniques up to date that they have something to contribute—and to build upon—in working directly with the public in deprived areas.

One of the aims of community development is to enable people to do without the community worker, and to do so by raising levels of social, economic and political competence. This is intended to be achieved through co-operation between the community worker and the people. Among the results should be a reduction of passive or bemused dependence on services or authority figures, expansion in the range of significant choices open to people, and a greater degree of control over resources, including power, in different areas of their lives.

In the same way, the explicit objectives of soci'

—especially, but not exclusively, in a community development or community action setting—should include enabling people as far as possible to do without outside, professional research workers. It is ironic that while so many social researchers claim to be radical (ranging from reformist to revolutionary), they have done little to question or recast their traditional roles which are fundamentally elitist in character.

By comparison with their community work colleagues operating in the same setting, researchers typically play the part of expert outsiders, seeking to retain some 'proper' degree of professional detachment. They do not generally go out of their way to dispel the faint haze of mystery veiling their activities and purposes, or to explain what exactly happens to the material they gather so assiduously.

There is frequent criticism that the education, training, and social background of social workers, community workers, and administrators create a gap between them and those they are meant to assist, and this cultural gap widens as they proceed further down the social scale in their contacts and dealings with people. The cultural and, thus, the understanding gap grows as deprivation increases. Social researchers are handicapped by their approach, manner, accent, vocabulary, and image. If they want to close the social and cultural gap they will have to take the initiative.

Research workers need not wait for the deprived and inarticulate or their representatives to make the first approach. It is unlikely that such an approach will be made anyway—not least because even if they know of a research worker's existence (which most people will not) they are not likely to be aware that he has anything to offer that is relevant to their needs. Their image of the research worker, if they have one at all, will probably conform to a stereotype of some courteously remote individual—possibly glittering earnestly through spectacles, smiling through a beard, if male, or, if female, being confused with a charming sixth-former out on a 'project'. Whatever the image, the interviewer will be remembered as asking questions, noting replies on a clipboard or recording them invisibly on tape, but giving nothing away. Research workers sometimes seek to reassure interviewees by telling them that they will not appear as people in any report which will be written (sometime, somewhere) but as statistics or as anonymous utterers of sayings—duly classified to illustrate some general point as yet unformulated.

The givers of interview time and yielders of information will almost certainly not see the final report (unless they happen to buy it, if published), neither is it likely that they will be invited to comment on it in draft. Nor will they be asked to consider its implications or recommendations, even though these might deal with matters of burning concern to their lives.

Community researchers have been remarkably slow to recognise their obligations to the people who supply the information and about whom they draw conclusions embracing needs, opportunities, priorities and resources—ranging from intimate personal or family matters to structural, long-term economic or social changes affecting large numbers of people, possibly for generations. This is almost invariably done without consultation or mandate—or no more than the prospective mandate of the compassionate, humanitarian, but self-appointed observer.

Researchers should acknowledge that—however benign the intent—this kind of position, with the superior–subordinate status relationship which forms its axis, can be only justified as a temporary or first-stage one. It should lead on to measures designed to raise the status of people-as-research-objects in the research situation and, simultaneously, to achieve their real participation in the research process.

Where their work brings them into contact with or focuses upon people who are socially, economically, or politically deprived—and the three usually go together—a number of positive roles are open to researchers besides the traditional one. Without prostituting themselves they can assist the community by utilising experience and skills in ways that are educational, consultative, facilitating, supporting, and political.

The defects of the present situation are magnified by virtue of the fact that the poor, deprived, inarticulate or others of low status are treated differently by research workers from administrators, industrialists, professional people, or departments of local and central government. Deference applies in social research as in other fields. Those who possess power and status are likely to require—and get—'consultation', sometimes with veto rights, at draft stage before research findings are seen by a wider audience. The reasons for requiring this measure of control over the fruits of research may be no more sinister than a desire to ensure the maximum feasible degree of factual accuracy and balance of opinion. And while they might suspect that other motives are at play, most research workers would probably concede that the consultation requirement was reasonable.

Reasonable or not, the facility is not normally offered to ordinary people in deprived areas—or elsewhere. It might be revealing to test the reactions of research workers to a proposal that the poor should be granted the same access to, and influence upon, research findings as, say, local officials or civil servants.

While the introduction of consultation with 'the community' might slow down the processes of refinement and presentation—though that is by no means inevitable—it could also be expected to yield greater benefits, both by contributing to a sharpening of aims, methods and techniques, and by enhancing the validity and relevance of research material.

Inviting the participation of local people need not be restricted to the later stages of production in the research process. Nor should it be confined to consultation over a draft report. For although the exercise would be an advance on the traditional way of conducting research—which is in direct line of descent from Charles Booth and Seebohm Rowntree—it would still be heavily lopsided. As conceivers, parents, and guardians of their projects, and having gone through the agonies of preparing the hopefully mature results for public approbation, researchers understandably develop possessive and defensive feelings about their work. Discussion at that late stage incorporates some of the built-in disadvantages of consultation between planners and public over an already prepared—though 'provisional'—plan which the planners hope will be acclaimed by the people. The basis for genuine consultation is unlikely to exist in such a situation, and it will require an unusual degree of altruism—as well as diplomatic skill—on the part of the planners (researchers) to get both sides on equal footing. The authors of the plan (report) might have to be prepared to make major, even fundamental, concessions. But, whether or not they are (or believe they are) prepared to make changes to their masterpieces (using the term in its original sense), as exponents of the plan/research report they tend to determine the structure and course of discussion during the period of consultation, and speak from prepared positions which they will be loth to vacate.

The case for involving residents in identifying issues, formulating measures, conducting activities, handling resources, monitoring and evaluating processes and results is just as tenable in relation to community research as it is in community development. It is erroneous to perpetuate the assumption that community development can be prompted only through a constellation of activities labelled 'community work' or something like that.

Whatever the research theologians may assert, real-world experience teaches us that there is no clear or fixed line of demarcation between two sets of activities called, respectively, 'community work' and 'social research' (or 'community research'). They overlap to varying degrees and draw upon a common pool of knowledge and skills. Fact-gathering, observation, rational formulation of aims and methods, and reliable ways of testing the validity of results—whether of success or failure—are essential processes in good community work of all kinds, ranging from the most consensual to the most militant, and in good research of all kinds, ranging from rapid, one-off micro-studies to long-term programmes of macro-research. 'Applied commonsense' is probably the most useful tool in both research and community work.

It should not be overlooked by those researchers whose field of operations is out in the community that they are engaged in a social activity in which they are actors in a dynamic network of relationships. The closer the researchers' contacts with local people and their problems and hopes—particularly where this is through interviews or group sessions—the greater the blurring of the distinction over time between outsider (researcher) and locals. Though still limited, assimilation is likely to be greater when researchers make extensive use of informal methods of interviewing and participant observation. Moreover, the longer they work in a locality, the more do researchers become part of the local scene.

Thus, while it may pay allegiance to academic traditions, owe a great deal to abstract conceptualisation, make use of intricate formulae and electronic machinery back at base, research conducted in a community setting is a concrete activity performed by flesh-and-blood people who affect and are affected by those with whom they come into contact. It is an elementary requirement in community research that researchers should recognise the implications of their role and location and take them into account in carrying out their work. Some fail to do this adequately, others parade the illusion that they are scientists in a laboratory of inert specimens. For both categories of researcher, the result is almost certain to be distortion in research findings and, hence, in the conclusions derived from them.

Once researchers acknowledge the realities in the environment in which they are working, they can be more confident in examining the scope of their own potential roles in that environment. The discipline and ideals of scientific training (rationality, honesty, objectivity), may be invaluable, but the methods of research cannot always be transferred unaltered to a field situation when human beings are the research object of study, still less where they are active participants (as respondents) in the research.

Social researchers can contribute more extensively to community development (or social improvement) by exploring more flexible and radical ways of working—without this eroding their professional standards and ethics.

Conclusions

The potential utility to the community of certain features of the research approach have already been touched upon, but a number of other points are germane in considering how to make research more directly useful. We should first recognise that any utilitarian value of social research lies more in what it adds to people's knowledge, understanding, and competence and less in what it adds to the store of academic or theoretical wisdom. In the context of a deprived community, raising levels of 'competence' entails increasing people's political, economic, and social capabilities, i.e. the extent of self-determination and control in vital aspects of their daily lives.

Effective research proceeds from—and by means of—a series of related questions, and, as a generalisation, the more relevant and significant the questions are, the more useful will be the results. In order for a community to develop its capabilities and operate more effectively research workers should play a parallel role to that of community workers—encouraging, educating, supporting, acting as catalysts. Clearly, where there are community workers on the spot there should be co-operation and sharing of functions between them and researchers. Where there are no community workers, researchers can still take initiatives. They should do so, however, on the foundation of their own experience as research workers and not as community workers with neither training nor systematic experience.

Using their particular approach and experience, research workers can help to shape the analytical framework and the intelligence network to be used and improved by residents in pursuing their community action objectives. It is important, for instance, to help the community to develop the know-how so as to be able to analyse its own situation. This would involve examining the characteristics of the local economic, political and social structures; the nature and adequacy of resources available to the community; identifying problems; determining and articulating aspirations; formulating strategies based on an informed consideration of priorities and alternatives.

They would need to find out where and how the power was wielded, where the pressure points were in the local power structures, how local structures interlocked with larger ones, how the processes of decision-making operate and how to manipulate them.

Among the key questions which research workers can help to formulate and answer are:

1 What are the key issues as perceived by members of the community?
2 What are the causes which give rise to these issues?
3 To what extent are they due to organisational and policy factors in
   — local, central, or regional government?
   — industry (or other fields of employment)?
4 To what extent are the causes of key issues or problems generated by
   — social and economic conditions (including lack or imbalance of resources)?
   — the structure and functioning of the community itself?
   — inter-personal or inter-group relations?
5 How can the situation be changed?

Analyses, fact-gathering, and the dissemination of information can be conducted in various ways by residents. The establishment of a variety of groups concerned with the collection, examination and distribution would tend to raise overall effectiveness. The range of groups could include:[2] information and opinion centres; interviewing teams drawn from panels of residents carrying out *ad hoc* or rolling surveys; working parties focusing on particular issues (e.g. housing, transport, environment, pollution, consumer affairs, old people, children, education); a network of street or block committees or working parties linked up with district and area organisations; ethnic associations; tenants' or residents' associations; trade unions and trades councils; church groups; community relations councils; councils of social service; CAB; school groups; students' community groups; community newspapers; university or other extension and extra-mural groups; and so on. All of these are both suppliers and consumers of information, they are also important components in the community structure. That structure could be further strengthened to the advantage of the local people if community councils[3] were set up. They, too, would need 'research' material, and, reciprocally, would be one of the sources of information for community groups.

Among the potential benefits to residents of increasing the volume and variety of research and intelligence activity (with the assistance of professional research workers) would be:

  – a freer flow of significant information
  – a cumulative build-up of useful contacts, thereby strengthening the local social network
  – the evolution of a common consciousness of conditions, problems, dissatisfactions, aspirations
  – the fostering of a shared desire to do something about it
  – the emergence of leaders at different levels and representing a range of skills and functions.

The residents will remain behind after researchers and community workers have left—though they should be able and encouraged to call upon specialist services or advice when necessary. Access to authoritative, specialised information and judgments is, after all, one of the most potent advantages possessed by the middle class over the working class, or of the educated, articulate and wealthy over the ill-educated, inarticulate and poor. The advantages of the rich and the disadvantages of the poor are compounded by their respective knowledge of and abilities to exploit the systems which control the distribution of information and other resources.

Because the majority of people identify themselves with the district they live in there is, at the minimum, a potential incentive for them to find out more about how to tackle its deficiencies and problems. There is clearly enormous scope, as yet scarcely explored, for research workers—and the institutions that employ them—to play a part in stimulating awareness, passing on skills, and providing support to residents. It will be interesting, and significant, to see how researchers respond to the rising pressures for more effective popular participation in the political system and freer access to sources of information. Social researchers could make a major contribution—but will they?

References

1 See, for example, S. Town, 'Action research and social policy', *Sociological Review*, 21 (4), 1973, pp. 573–98; R. Rapoport, 'Three dilemmas in action research', *Human Relations*, 23 (6), 1970, pp. 499–513; A. H. Halsey, *Educational Priority*, vol. 1, HMSO, 1972, chapter 12. Each of these three authors reviews the literature on action-research but from differing points of view, thus providing three complementary perspectives.

2 A background paper prepared by Marjorie Mayo for the UN Study Group on Community Development and Urban Deprivation, Oxford, September 1972, describes the impressive variety of community groups and organisations. It also contains appendices listing the names and addresses of agencies which can provide further information. The paper has now been published by the National Council of Social Service. Another informative source, describing the activities and strategy of the Shelter Neighbourhood Action Project in Liverpool, is to be found in *Another Chance for Cities*, Shelter, 1972, especially sections 3, 4 and 5.

3 There are several neighbourhood councils in London and some other cities, while recent Local Government Acts make provision for community councils in Scotland and a new style of parish councils in England. The powers of such councils are circumscribed and their functions are largely consultative, but within the restricted framework there is scope for strengthening local representation and involvement. Information about neighbourhood councils and their activities—not to be confused with the prospective community and parish councils as defined in legislation—may be obtained from Association for Neighbourhood Councils, 18 Victoria Park Square, London, E.2.

Part V   Consumer Organisations

13 The Mental Patients' Union

Liz Durkin and Brian Douieb

An individual having unusual difficulties in coping with his environment struggles and kicks the dust, as it were. I have used the figure of a fish caught on a hook: his gyrations must look peculiar to other fish that don't understand the circumstances; but his splashes are not his affliction and, as every fisherman knows, these efforts may succeed (Karl Mennenger).

The theoretical background of the Union

Mental patients are one of the most subtly oppressed groups in this society. Labelled by psychiatry and the medical profession 'psychopath', 'schizophrenic', 'character disorder', etc., the patient is refused the most basic rights, legally by the Mental Health Act 1959 and professionally by psychiatry, and is invalidated as a human being. He is punished for any attempt to be himself, as opposed to what society wants him to be, by brain surgery, electric shock, drugs and confinement in hospital—all under the guise of 'treatment' and 'benevolence'.

The desperate need for a union of mental patients and ex-patients to combat the increasingly repressive institution of psychiatry and to fight for even the most basic human rights denied them was the call of the pamphlet 'The need for a mental patients' union'.[1] Written by the pilot committee for a Mental Patients' Union, an *ad hoc* committee of mental patients and ex-patients set up in December 1972, it took the view that 'psychiatry is one of the most subtle methods of repression in advanced capitalist society'. It asserted a direct link between psychiatry and class repression—'the heavy weapon of psychiatry, like many others, is held at the heads of the working class in order to control them.' Figures show that proportionately more admissions to mental hospitals originate from areas of poverty, bad housing, high unemployment and heavy industry—*in short, working-class areas.*

As the committee pointed out, workers are forced at times to react as individuals against the boredom, sterility and virtual slavery of their work function within society. Alienated from their labour, appendages of mass production machinery or aimless producers of socially useless products, trapped in the breadwinner role between family and job, it is hardly surprising that a man who has worked on a production line for years can become increasingly depressed and eventually regard himself as 'a machine', a 'robot', 'controlled by something outside of himself'; by 'voices telling him what to do'. He expresses in apparent 'fantasy' the reality of his alienation from himself and the fact that he is controlled by his work situation and his place in the socio-economic system. Yet psychiatry labels him 'psychotic', and prescribes drugs or electric shock treatment to destroy his thought patterns and to numb his mind. These 'treatments' invalidate him further as a human being; he is not allowed even his individual reaction to the situation. For psychiatry to acknowledge these reactions as 'reasonable' would be for it to accept that the causes of the reactions need changing, i.e. the nature of the profit system. But the rulers of society, those with power and wealth, are interested only in concealing these causes and preventing social unrest. This con-trick is carried out by its agents, the psychiatrists. The role of psychiatry to suppress opponents of capitalism by medical treatment is illustrated by recent statements that workers who strike are 'mentally ill', and suggestions regarding the establishment of psychiatric clinics in factories.

Social (and political) deviants are punished for being different from 'normal' people (or attempts are made to 'rehabilitate' them to 'normality'), in a society where normality is to be a robot on a production line; to compete against other human beings in the survival of the fittest; to cope in appalling poverty, begging for social security (social insecurity); and to live in high-rise boxes or rat-infested slums. The definition of normality must be challenged; after all, 'is not the individual who functions normally, adequately and healthily as a citizen of a sick society—is not such an individual himself sick?'[2]

The pamphlet points out the particular position of women. They not only suffer the same work conditions as men, often for lower pay, but are expected to act as slaves to their husbands and children.

It is hardly surprising that the figures show that one in six women go into mental hospitals at some point in their lives compared to one in nine men—how many more are outpatients of a psychiatric clinic or receive drugs from their GP? The very fact that the numbers 'needing treatment' are so great surely reflects the nature of this society.

Another road to psychiatric treatment is unemployment. The pamphlet describes the process:

> When workers are no longer useful to the capitalist economy (i.e. their labour value is lost), they are thrown onto the human scrap heap like useless pieces of machinery. Unemployment directly benefits capitalism, since it discourages industrial action for better working conditions and wages, KEEPING PROFITS HIGH AND BIG BUSINESS HAPPY. Meanwhile the state conveniently covers for the system by blaming unemployment on pay inflation but is left with the responsibility of keeping the anger of the Trade Unions down at the increasing numbers of unemployed. So the system quickly attaches the labels of 'lazy' and 'inadequate' to some mystical proportion of the unemployed through its propaganda media,—however, this method no longer suffices to dupe the more organised sections of the working class. But at the same time in increasing use, is a more effective method which subtly stigmatises the worker (now a 'deviant' because he does not work)—he is labelled 'mentally ill'. This is not difficult to do because by this stage the unemployed worker is beginning to feel the bite, since he is not fulfilling his breadwinner role and the pressures within the family are increasing. He also feels frustration at not finding a job, and humiliation and victimisation in claiming social security. However, the immediacy of the family's needs makes it difficult for it to sustain the drop in living standards and the family blames him for its hardship rather than the system. In this way he becomes the scapegoat for the economics of capitalism which have deliberately created the pool of unemployment in which he is trapped. Crushed beneath the mounting pressures he becomes depressed, disillusioned and aimless. The psychiatrist does the rest!

Furthermore, the so-called welfare state collides with this concept of 'deviancy' in order to protect the interests of capitalism. A particularly vicious piece of recent legislation, the 1973 Social

Security Act, states that unless a mental patient agrees with and undergoes prescribed psychiatric treatment, his benefit may be withdrawn. This means that he is forced into the position where he has no choice—he must be 'treated' or starve. However, as the pamphlet points out, the middle class is not exempt from falling foul of capitalism.

> As the managers, administrators and apologists for capitalism, the middle class is obliged to defer to the ideology of its masters, the ruling class of money-barons. In order to preserve its status and security of economic privilege and the tenuous distinction between itself and the working class, the middle class must maintain reactionary values. Those members of the middle class who offend against, reject, or who are unable to cope with the values of alienated individualism (squalid private mentality), competitiveness, and 'striving for success', are seen as a threat to the class values and therefore the class position. 'Deviants' expressing their escape from or attack of the class values through 'depression', 'psychosis' or 'character disorder', having been thus labelled, add to the numbers conveniently dealt with by psychiatry.

The middle-class 'deviant' confronted by psychiatry is thrown into the relationship of the worker versus the ruling class.

To protect the *status quo* and to maintain the profits of the rich, the 'deviant' is scapegoated as the problem in need of treatment. This process of victim-blaming is used to persuade the patient that he himself, not the system, is at fault. He is encouraged to see his symptoms as a distorted reaction to 'reality' (as defined by the psychiatrist, of course), he is, therefore, in need of 'adjustment'. In this way the nature of the 'reality' is unquestioned. W. Ryan[3] describes this process, and shows that 'just as the poor are blamed for their poverty, the unemployed for their idleness, slum tenants for their housing conditions, and "backward" schoolchildren for their "backwardness"', so the mental patient is blamed for his 'illness'.

The formation and aims

The pilot committee distributed posters to mental hospitals, day centres and hostels advertising a meeting to be held at Paddington Day Hospital on 21 March 1973. They wanted to ensure that the meeting was one of mental patients, not professionals, and their efforts paid off. Over 150 people attended, of whom over 100 were patients or ex-patients. Some had travelled from as far afield as Leeds, Birmingham and Southampton; there were patients from hospitals ranging from Broadmoor and Shenley to therapeutic communities. The latter were least aware of the urgent need for a union, as they felt that they were in a less repressive position than those inside large hospitals. In particular, those in units with patients' committees believed themselves to have power already although they were challenged by other patients as to the real extent of their power. It became apparent that this did not extend to seeing their own casenotes, being able to discharge themselves or having control of the unit.

It was decided almost immediately at the meeting that only mental patients and ex-patients (including out-patients) could be full members of the union; others who supported the union could be associate members, but with no voting rights. Relatives of patients, it was decided, could not be full members, as patients said that relatives were frequently instrumental in hospitalising them and that they did not necessarily share the same interests as the patients. The meeting unanimously declared the formation of the national Mental Patients' Union, but decided that local groups should be set up which were to be autonomous. It was agreed to run the Union by subscriptions from members so that it would be self-supporting, and members in hospital particularly requested membership cards as they felt it important for patients inside institutions to have material means of identification and solidarity. The meeting also agreed on some aspects of a Declaration of Intent and arranged for these to be continued by a working party.

One member, Robin Farquarson, offered the Union the use of a house near King's Cross to set up as an office and some others went the next day to work on this squat with him. The first meeting of the working party was to be held there, but the following day Robin was injured in a fire and died ten days later. This was a severe blow to the Union in its first days. For a while, members continued to work on in the house but, as the organisation grew, there was not sufficient energy to cope with this. Meanwhile, another member offered another squat as an office and within three weeks of the meeting the M P U had an office.

Camden Council has now evicted the Union from their office in Camden. Following a campaign against the Social Services

Departments and pressure brought through publicity and involvement of the social workers, the Chairman of the Social Services Committee has promised the Union alternative premises without strings attached, arguing that the presence of the Union in Camden will provide an 'effective criticism of the Council's services'.

The working party consisted of twenty to thirty full members, most of whom had long experience in mental hospitals, who worked long hours after the first meeting to outline a Declaration of Intent which was later passed at the second General Meeting together with the organisational structure of the Union, as follows:[4]

> We proclaim the dignity of society's so-called mental patients.
>
> We CHALLENGE repressive psychiatric practice and its ill-defined concepts of 'mental illness'.
>
> We STATE that the present appalling situation in 'mental health' primarily arises from the ACUTE problems in HOUSING, UNEMPLOYMENT and SOCIAL INEQUALITY.
>
> MENTAL PATIENTS in our society are treated as people with NO HUMAN RIGHTS. We are STIGMATISED, and our accounts of what happens to us in mental hospitals and outside are taken as symptoms of an 'illness'. Most of us are never even given the opportunity to speak about what happens in mental hospitals, as we are incarcerated there and subjected to 'treatments' which DESTROY our MEMORIES, CONFUSE our SPEECH and CO-ORDINATION, DESTROY our INCENTIVE and INTIMIDATE us.
>
> OUR FIRST INTENT in forming ourselves into a UNION is to FIGHT against the 'CONSPIRACY of DEAFNESS' that confronts us.
>
> The MENTAL PATIENTS' UNION will REPRESENT mental patients wherever they require to be represented. WE WILL FIGHT to make what rights of representation formally exist effective and secure rights of representation wherever they do not exist. We will seek to INFORM patients and ex-patients about their RIGHTS, minimal though they are e.g. the right to appeal against compulsory detention in some circumstances). We will, however, as representatives of our fellow mental patients REFUSE to bargain behind the backs of our members with the 'authorities'. We will attempt to provide LEGAL, SOCIAL and ADVISORY SUPPORT for all mental patients and ex-patients who ask the Union for help.

WE WILL EXPOSE the MYTH that most treatment and admission to mental hospitals is really voluntary. We will do this by:

1. PUBLICISING the deceit that authorities use to get people into mental hospitals with the least resistance, the DECEPTION and FORCE that is frequently used to inflict 'treatment'; and the cases of forcibly detained patients classified as 'voluntary'.

2. EXPOSING the desperate SITUATIONS where people have no alternative but to accept mental hospital admission because of lack of accommodation, necessary welfare services or homes for the elderly.

3. EXPOSING the POWER of psychiatrists to prevent technically 'voluntary' patients from leaving by imposing compulsory detention orders, removing patients' clothes, by locking 'open' wards and by heavy drug use and other deceptive tactics.

We will expose the use of 'treatments' as forms of punishment.

We will expose the way in which Social Workers are USED as CONTROL AGENTS to cover up the social outrages of our society; and how industrial and occupational therapy is used as a source of CHEAP LABOUR, and expose the dull, SOUL-DESTROYING work which is called occupational therapy.

We intend to show how 'REHABILITATION' is used as a process which seeks only to achieve ADJUSTMENT and CONFORMITY of the patient to the PRESENT SOCIAL SYSTEM.

We will show how PSYCHOTHERAPY can act as a subtle form of social control.

WE DEMAND

the abolition of compulsory treatment; i.e. we demand the effective right of patients to refuse any specific treatment.

the abolition of any right of 'authorities' to treat patients in the face of opposition of relatives or closest friends unless it is clearly shown that the patient of his own volition desires the treatment.

the abolition of irreversible psychiatric 'treatments' (electro-convulsive therapy, brain surgery, specific drugs).

higher standards in the testing of 'treatments' before use on us.

that patients be told what 'treatments' they are receiving experimental and should have the effective right to refuse to be experimented on.

that patients to be told what 'treatments' they are receiving and what the long-term effects are.

also the abolition of isolation 'treatment' (seclusion in locked side rooms, padded cells, etc.)

the right of any patient to inspect his casenotes and the right to take legal action relating to the contents and consequences of them.

that the 'authorities' should not discharge a patient against his or her will because they refuse 'treatment' or for any other reason.

that all patients should have the right to have any 'treatment' which they believe will help them.

that local authorities should provide housing for patients wishing to leave hospital and that adequate security benefits should be provided. We will support any mental patients or ex-patients in their struggle to get these facilities and any person who is at risk of becoming a mental patient because of inadequate accommodation, financial support, social pressures, etc.

We call for the abolition of compulsory hospitalisation.

an end to the indiscriminate use of the term 'mental subnormality'. We intend to fight the condemnation of people as 'mentally subnormal' in the absence of any real practical work to tackle the problem with active social understanding and help.

the abolition of the concept of 'psychopath' as a legal or medical category.

the right of patients to retain their personal clothing in hospitals and to secure personal possessions without interference by hospital staff.

the abolition of compulsory work in hospitals and outside and the abolition of the right of hospital 'authorities' to withhold and control patients' money.

the right of patients to join and participate fully in the Trade Union of their choice.

that Trade Union rates are paid to patients for any work done where such rates do not yet exist.

that patients should have recourse to a room in which they

can enjoy their own privacy, or have privacy with others, of either sex, of their own choosing.

the abolition of censorship by hospital authorities of patients' communications with society outside the hospital and in particular the abolition of telephone and letter censorship. We demand the abolition of any power to restrict patients' visiting rights by the hospital 'authorities'.

the right of Mental Patients' Union representatives to inspect all areas of hospitals, or equivalent institutions.

We deny that there is any such thing as 'incurable' mental 'illness' and demand the right to investigate the circumstances of any mental hospital patient who believes he or she is being treated as 'incurable'.

We demand that every mental patient or ex-patient should have the right to a free second opinion by a psychiatrist of the patient's or Mental Patients' Union representatives' choice, if he or she disagrees with the diagnosis

and that every mental patient or ex-patient should have the right to effective appeal machinery.

We believe that the EVENTUAL ABOLITION of MENTAL HOSPITALS and the institution of REPRESSIVE AND MANIPULATIVE PSYCHIATRY is possible, but ONLY IF SOCIETY IS RADICALLY CHANGED, for what is known as 'MENTAL ILLNESS' IS A SYMPTOM OF A DEFECTIVE AND SICK SOCIETY.

Some professionals have said that the Union is controlled by a small group of 'politicos', and that these, in the main, wrote the Declaration of Intent. This is a tactic to invalidate the Union. Professionals do not like to believe that mental patients can organise effectively, because to do so would be to challenge their self-definition of being 'trained helpers'.

The organisational structure of the Union is such that all policy is agreed collectively at general meetings which must be held quarterly. Up until the third general meeting a working party, open to all full members, continued the work of the Union. As a result of this a network of committed people emerged to share the day-to-day functioning; these now comprise the co-ordinating committee, elected at the third general meeting, and subject to immediate recall. Different members have taken responsibility for particular areas of work, e.g. filing, printing, research, relationship with hospital

8

6 Liz Durkin and Brian Douieb

patients, relationship with the press and local groups. A co-ordinator is not a leader, but is purely someone who reminds the group that a task needs doing and is responsible for seeing that it gets done.

Professionals might feel that mental patients are vulnerable to being controlled but, on the contrary, mental patients have experienced so much control in the past, particularly by their families and also inside institutions, that they are extra sensitive to the needs of themselves and of each other. Each task in the Union requires the involvement of several members. Working together is a complex process. Members spend hours understanding each other in order that they can function together in solidarity. Their emotional involvement and commitment to each other is total. This, after all, is the meaning of the word 'union'. In single-issue campaigns, relationships can remain superficial but, in the Union, members are assisting each other in survival. Survival is not on just a physical basis, e.g. poverty, homelessness, but emotional—members, after all, have been invalidated as people. The Union has to build up trust between its members if they are to work collectively.

The Union also realises the importance of a structure that does not lay pressure on people to work within it. There must be no underlying guilt if a member does not attend meetings for a few weeks. Each member knows that others will give what they can and that that is all that is expected of him or her.

The co-ordinating committee has no control over the several local groups both inside and outside hospitals, which are autonomous and self-financing. In this way the Union is similar to the claimants' unions. At the general meetings it has been the declared policy that it is a grass-roots organisation, and that the most important part of its work must be at the local level, particularly inside the mental hospitals in confronting psychiatry at the point where it is practised.

The movement to form patients' organisations is international. Members of the MPU recently went to Paris for a European conference attended by patients' groups from France, Germany and Spain. They discussed the possibility of an International Declaration of Intent and joint action. There is soon to be another meeting with the Dutch groups. There is also close contact with the American and Canadian groups, representatives of which have already spent time working with the Union.

The Union is frequently challenged with two questions: 'Where can people go who are suffering?' and 'What happens to people who are violent?' To the first question, the Union realises that as long as this social structure remains, people will suffer, so in the short term it plans to set up houses run and controlled by patients as asylums, i.e. places of refuge but without treatment, therapy or hierarchies. To answer the second question, we have to evaluate what is meant by 'crimes of violence'. The 'crime of violence' being considered must be weighed in relation to other kinds of violence. People may well worry about others who rape young children or beat their wives, but the vast amount of violence that goes unpunished does not reach the headlines in the same way; e.g. the violence of war, poverty, torture, class exploitation and the daily persecution of mental patients inside hospitals. The media focus attention on individual cases to scapegoat the 'criminally insane' and to distract people from other real crimes that take place on a wider level. It can be argued that people who are defined as 'criminally insane' should be classified under the penal system. A man in prison has more rights than one in a mental hospital; at least he is entitled to a legal defence and has a sentence of a defined time. By mixing those labelled 'criminally insane' with other patients in mental hospitals, the public are led to fear all mental patients as dangerous and this increases the stigma. Apart from these arguments, many patients would claim that they can help someone who is violent because they understand the cause of this and the underlying reasons. It is no answer to treat violence with the violence of total isolation, electric shock, drugs and leucotomy.

Considering that the Union has been established only a year, it has grown steadily and is certainly disproving those who thought that mental patients as dangerous and this increases the stigma. Apart German patients' group says, 'We must make a weapon of our sickness'—and we intend to aim this weapon against not merely psychiatry but the social and economic causes of suffering.

The Union's opposition to social work

The M P U is a threat to both caseworkers and community workers. It challenges the basic concepts of social work theory and the use of the professional in achieving individual and social changes. Whilst casework is criticised for focusing on individual problems, community work is seen to be attacking the wider social and economic inequalities; yet by its methods it becomes another subtle method of oppression and a justification for professional intervention in the lives of the oppressed. The professional caseworker or community worker assumes the position of knowledge, expertise and skill in assisting 'deviants'; whether, according to the consensus model, they help them to adjust to their situation, or whether, according to the conflict model, they help them to fight against it, the precept is still that of helping the underprivileged, and the nature of this intervention is in itself paternalistic, manipulative and oppressive.

Professionals are agents of repression. Professionals make their living out of those who are oppressed. It is a necessary part of their existence that they define their clients as 'abnormal' in order to preserve their own 'normality', and, therefore, their own financial and status positions.

Whether psychiatrist, caseworker or community worker, the professional sees the client as a client. The client thus defined is powerless. In traditional psychiatry, he loses even the most basic human rights once this labelling process has taken place.

One member of the Union expresses his view as follows:

> They lock you up and they drive you insane
> And then they cunningly pick at your brain
> And all the time they're treating you well
> Their form of torture is cruel as hell.
> They don't want to cure you—you keep them in jobs
> You keep them in power—they must feel like gods.
> And when you meet them, you can't help but smile
> They're always so nice on the surface, their style
> Is 'We want to help you' and they really believe
> That they want to help you, but they won't let you leave,
> The whole situation is really quite bad
> If they believe their delusions, then they must be mad!

The psychiatrist is seen to have medical expertise. This gives him the power to enforce any medical treatment without the patient's permission that he considers to be in the patient's 'best interests'. The patient, even if voluntary, can be given irreversible brain surgery, electric shock treatment or paralytic drugs; he can be incarcerated on a locked ward or totally isolated, and if he objects it can be said that 'he cannot decide for himself'. In what ways can he refute medical opinion? If the doctors say it is a disease, how can he argue? Many patients will accept the opinion because they are desperate and bewildered and conditioned into accepting professional advice. Social workers try to rehabilitate the patients to help them adjust back into 'normality'. They encourage the patient to go to industrial centres to do monotonous work for little or no wages in an attempt to push them back into a mode of production which may well have precipitated the 'illness'. They send patients from hospital to 'halfway houses' to 'get them on their feet' and after six months they again have to face an accommodation situation of extortionate rents and overcrowding. They encourage patients to take tablets which repress their feelings, so that they can cope in a situation they were reacting against. They give psychotherapy to brainwash the patient into seeing the problem within his personality and accepting the evils of the system. If the patient is not successfully rehabilitated, social workers facilitate the containment of the 'deviant' in the dustbins of society, the mental hospitals, where through treatment and isolation he can be physically and mentally destroyed.

It is the nature of the professional relationship that the professionals have the power. They maintain a position of authority by mystifying the patient and claiming expertise about his condition by the use of jargon he doesn't understand and by getting him to expose his feelings—but never revealing theirs; by these means they repress the patient by taking control of his life out of his hands. If the patient does not act submissively and with 'respect', he is soon labelled 'demanding, manipulative, or psychopathic'; it is expected that he should be co-operative and 'adjusted to his situation'.

What then is the role of the community worker in this field? The professional community worker is no different from other professionals. He claims to have an expertise which he can use to help the client group negotiate the power structure and he may advise them on appropriate tactics and strategies. By assuming this position the client group remain in a powerless position. The presence of a community worker in such a group reinforces their dependent position. Paul Freire[5] points this out: 'Self deprecation is a characteristic of the oppressed which derives from their internalisation of the opinion the oppressors have of them, so often do they hear they are good for nothing, know nothing and are incapable of learning anything, that they are sick, lazy and unproductive.' He also says: 'If agents of the oppressor class join the oppressed in their struggle they almost always bring with them the marks of their origin, their prejudices and deformations, which include a lack of confidence in the people's ability to think, to want and to know . . . they talk about the people but they do not trust them.'[6]

The community worker will say, like the caseworker, that he adheres to the principle of client self-determination. In casework, the social worker will allow the client to make his own decisions as long as these coincide with his. At the point when the social worker disagrees, the client will be labelled, so that what he says is invalidated. Ray Lees says of community action:[7] 'There are problems in bringing groups together in this way. The conflict has to be recognized, but the groups also have to be well organized and well intentioned so as to avoid extremism and possible violence.' It would appear that the community group can only take such action as the community worker decides to be permissible. If he is employed by the authority which the group is attacking, then it can be assumed that the limitations of action will be great!

What claim have the professionals to expertise? How much can they comprehend of human suffering when socially, geographically and economically they are far removed from the needs of their 'clients'? It is the oppressed themselves who have experienced their situation and who know best how to organise to fight their oppression. Paul Freire suggests the direction for the professional.[8]

> Discovering himself to be an oppressor may cause considerable anguish but it does not necessarily lead to solidarity with the oppressed. Rationalising his guilt through paternalistic treatment of the oppressed all the while holding them in a position of dependence will not do. Solidarity requires that one enter into the situation of those with whom one is identifying . . . true solidarity with the oppressed means fighting at their side.

The MPU has rejected the role of the professional and is, therefore, controlled by mental patients. Any professional who supports its aims is to some extent expressing a contradiction. But those who wish to help the Union may fight under the control of patients. They must recognise the importance of mental patients fighting their own struggles, learning from their own direct experience of conflict—this is vital if the Union is to dispel accusations that its members are too 'ill' to be able to organise.

The new careers scheme for 'mental patients' and 'ex-criminals' whereby they are employed in the social services, appears at first sight to be anti-professional and progressive. However, this is a devious method of absorbing the voice of dissent into the establishment by offering temptation of local government salaries and status. It is also a question of 'divide and rule', as by working with the professionals, new careerists become alienated and removed from other members of their oppressed group. Furthermore they can provide an often cheap method of doing the dirty work of social workers, as their assistants. Politicians are currently begging for the participation of workers in industry—community work seeks the clients' participation but not control. Client control is as threatening to the power structure as workers' control. The Union will not be 'bought out' by seemingly well-meaning councils or voluntary organisations.

The Mental Patients' Union is a desperately needed organisation at a time when psychiatry is increasingly being used as an instrument of social, economic and political repression. It remains to be seen what the 'official' reaction will be towards it.

References

1 Pilot committee for a mental patients' union, 'The Need for a Mental Patients' Union' (unpublished paper).
2 H. Marcuse, *Eros and Civilisation*, Sphere Paperback, 1970.
3 W. Ryan, *Blaming the Victim*, Orbach & Chambers, 1971, p. 136
4 Mental Patients' Union, 'Declaration of Intent' (copies available from 37 Mayola Road, London E5).
5 Paul Freire, *The Pedagogy of the Oppressed*, Penguin, 1972. p. 38.
6 Ibid., p. 36.
7 R. Lees, *Politics and Social Work*, Routledge & Kegan Paul, 1972, p. 82.
8 Freire, op. cit., p. 26.

14 Camden old age pensioners

Betty Harrison

The author has been a full-time trade union official for twenty-five years, first in the Fire Brigades Union for seven years and from 1946 to 1964 in the Tobacco Workers' Union. As a national organiser at a time when very few women reached a national position in any job, Betty says she 'had to work twice as hard as a man to prove she was half as good'—but she and the women in other trade union jobs fought their way through these prejudices. Since retirement, Betty has been very active in the old age pensioners' movement. She has been treasurer of the Camden Old Age Pensioners' and Trade Union Action Association, and claims that her trade union experience has been invaluable in her work in the old age pensioners' movement. This article is based on an interview with Marjorie Mayo for the Editorial Board.

Could you describe how the branches of the Old Age Pensioners' Union were set up and organised in Camden?

We held a meeting in the Town Hall, where a lot of people came, and we signed them up. We agreed that we should make a charge of 5p a year. We then had to go out to try and get members in other ways. The first meeting was organised by the Camden Trades Council and Camden Borough Council. The Trades Council invited people and I think that there were almost more Trades Council people and Labour Councillors there than pensioners. The information had also gone round by word of mouth, and we had a few names and addresses of people who were interested.

We then went to luncheon clubs and talked to people, many of whom joined. Then, during the summer of 1972, some members stood outside the Post Office in Kentish Town. Those who lived in the Regent's Park area had an easier job because there is a big estate there and they could go round to the houses and flats.

But in Kentish Town we couldn't do it quite like that so we stood outside the Post Office on the days when the pensioners went to draw their money, and gave out duplicated forms. The first part of these forms said who and what we were, and what our objectives were; the bottom part was an application to join, and we signed some of them up there and then outside the Post Office. One of our members in Kentish Town then had the idea of asking the Consumer Aid Association in Kentish Town Road to lend us a table and a chair. This particular fellow sat there several days a week, and others went and helped too. Sometimes we had people lining up to sign on. When we had quite a number of addresses on these forms, we called a local meeting in Kentish Town. We found that some of the people who signed belonged to the Holly Lodge Estate, so we got in touch with one of the men up there who had come to the first of our meetings and gave him the names and addresses of the people from that area who had joined, and he formed a branch there. We then wrote to all our local Kentish Town addresses, which added up to over a hundred people, and asked them to come to a meeting. We had been given permission by the Director of Social Services in Camden to use Social Service Centres, and the Leighton Road Centre agreed to let us have our meeting there. On this particular occasion, we posted the notices, and out of over a hundred people we got forty-seven to the first meeting—from that we more or less formed our Kentish Town branch. I must add that on my initiative we didn't make it into a formal branch. I have found that if you have these organisations with a chairman and secretary, the rest of the members tend to sit back and let those three or four people do all the work. We don't to this day have a committee; all problems are raised at the full branch meeting and everybody takes part in discussing them. I agreed that I would more or less guide these meetings without actually being chairman, and that if there was any correspondence, I would do it. We have gone on like that ever since.

Now some of the other branches have been organised in different ways. The Regent's Park branch, for instance, found it much easier to organise themselves, for the reason I have already mentioned; there is also a community centre on the estate, where they held their first meeting. They formed their branch formally with a chairman and secretary and treasurer. And if that's their way of working, well that's all right, too, although I think personally that they get less participation from the majority of their members than we do.

Then Task Force and the Neighbourhood Centre in Malden Road started to form a branch in that particular area. They took a leaf out of our book and went outside the Post Offices and they had one or two big blocks of flats which they could canvass for members. They called a meeting at the Neighbourhood Centre and asked me to go and speak when their branch was formed. Here again, they had a chairman and secretary and a committee, and within a fortnight half the committee resigned, which meant there were only two people left; then the chairman had to give up because he fell ill, so they were left with no one in the way of officials. But they were still determined in wanting a branch, so they found a new chairman and secretary, and at the present time perhaps fifteen or so people go fairly regularly.

Local branches have been formed all over north-west London now, and I have been along to speak to them. The only trouble as far as I am concerned is that because I am articulate and have some experience of organisation through my trade union background, anybody who's starting up a new branch wants me to go and talk to them, and this has meant quite a bit of work. But most of these new branches have got off the ground now, with one exception. The Task Force people had spoken to the organiser, who was in charge of a lunch club at the Maiden Lane Community Site, and so we too went along to speak there. Task Force showed a couple of very useful films they had made of interviews with two or three old people, and then I spoke. We got about seventeen people interested who wanted to have a chairman and secretary and form a committee and, as far as I knew, they were going to go on all right. The next thing I learned was that the whole branch had collapsed. When I enquired—and this is only hearsay as I didn't experience it myself—I found that the Claimants' Union had gone there to talk to them. Apparently they had not understood, being in the main young people, what old people are like and how they respond to things. Because they had made a fighting speech about making claims and making appeals on their claims and all this kind of thing, the old people were terrified by this, as they could see themselves constantly in tribunals or something; so they shied away from the whole thing. I think also, although I don't want to be harsh about it, that the organiser in charge at Maiden Lane wasn't all that enamoured of either the Claimants' Union or the OAPs' Association, but preferred to keep the luncheon club as a purely social organisation not connected in any way with any other organisation, especially a militant one. Anyway, for whatever reason, that Maiden Lane branch is one of the failures that we've had.

How do you recruit new members, and how do you organise the meetings to keep up their interest and active participation?

We keep getting new members all the time: not so much by standing outside shops and post offices: in the winter, anyway, old people can't really be expected to do that: but by people who are already members bringing in their neighbours and friends. One of the things we've done in our Kentish Town branch, which I think has kept the branch going very healthily, is that we have had a succession of speakers on various subjects. One evening a young man brought some folk records along which we enjoyed very much: but we've had serious speakers, too. For instance, when people have talked about problems with social security, I suggested that we ask the manager of the local Social Security office in Kentish Town to come and speak to us. Well, he did, and gave us a very good lecture. Then, of course, our people were able to tell him of our difficulties with Social Security. There was the case of two of our members, a very nice and dignified old couple now nearly eighty. They both have a pension, because the wife worked, so she doesn't only have the pension for a wife, but her own pension which is the same amount of money as her husband receives. At that time it was £6.75 each. They had no other income. I think they had a small amount of savings, but by the time you are eighty those have nearly disappeared, anyway. At the beginning of last winter they wanted some new blankets and we advised them to go down to the Social Security, so they went. The young man behind the counter asked what was their income. They told him that they had £6.75 each, and he said: 'What? On £13 you don't need to come here—you've more than enough to live on.' The old couple were so upset they just left and now they won't go near the place again. This is the kind of attitude which not all, but still some of them, have in social security work: that people who go there are all trying to get something for nothing. Our people have paid for it themselves through their insurance and they are very sensitive on this point. They have never had to beg for things before.

Can I ask you whether it is more difficult to organise older people because they are less mobile, and, if so, how you cope with that problem?

Yes, this is a problem. You see, we don't have the same people coming now as when we first started. The same number come, and some of these are original members who have kept coming, but the membership changes because old people get so that they can't come out, some of them go into hospital for various things, and some of them die. But we have tried to keep in touch with all our members, whether they can come to meetings or not. There's one woman whose husband died a few months back, for instance; some of our OAPs went along to the funeral and then brought her to the branch, because she didn't want to come on her own at first. Now she comes regularly because she feels that we are her friends. Anyone who is sick or in hospital we will make a collection for, and then two of our women go down to see them. We have found that it is our women who mostly go out to see people and this kind of thing. Although we have a large number of men members, they don't fancy going to hospital to see a sick woman. Our members also keep in touch with their neighbours, and this is one reason why they keep bringing neighbours along to join. We do have a steady flow of new members, usually two or three at each branch, so that we are growing all the time. If we have to call a special meeting to discuss any particular problem, we get out a circular—I usually do that—but we don't have to post it. I give a bunch of notices to various people in different parts of the area we cover and they deliver them in person. Now when they deliver them, they don't just put them through the door; they usually take the opportunity to ring the bell and talk to the people and say: 'You haven't been to the meetings recently; are you sick or something, or do you need some help, or should we call for you?' So we have a whole social network, and this is very beneficial to our members. For instance, one woman who hasn't been to the meetings for some time because of illness rang me up yesterday. She has a problem about which she is really desperate. She lives in a Council flat in Lawford Road, and has been without hot water for two months now. Hot water is very essential to this woman because she's something wrong with her legs, and she ought to be able to steep them in hot water every night. I tried to get hold of one of the Councillors for this area, but he wasn't available, so I'll have to try again this evening. This is the kind of problem we try to take up for our members.

Incidentally, because we had so many problems to do with housing, I asked the Housing Director if he could come to discuss them with us. He wrote back to say that he didn't think it was the job of a Council official, and that what I wanted was a Councillor. So I wrote to the Chairman of the Housing Committee, who sent a deputy—one of the Councillors for this area. Fortunately for our members, he is also chairman of the Housing Services Committee, so they were able to ask him various things, and he was a great help to one of our members who had had an unfortunate experience with some Council workmen.

Out of all these issues you take up, could you rank them in order of their importance for your organisation?

Well, all these social problems, however important in themselves, are incidental to the main work of the organisation. The main issues are usually connected with housing—lack of hot water, workmen taking weeks to come along and do repairs—but the real issue is lack of money. Our main aim is to increase the pensions of old people, with the ultimate objective of getting a pension related to the average earnings in industry. One has to be careful that it's the average earnings and not the average wage, because there is a vast difference. A man in the motor industry, for instance, might earn £40 or £50 a week; but if you brought it down to his actual wage, it might be £20. So we want two-thirds of the average male earnings in the country. We are working for this because we want to do away with people going to Social Security to ask for the money to buy another blanket. We don't want them to have to ask for the telephone to be paid for, either, or the television licence. All these demands are also in our programme. But we are different from other organisations such as Care for the Elderly and Good Neighbours because we don't want these things as charity or handouts. We feel that the old age pensioner has earned them as a right, particularly this generation of o a p s who fought and won two World Wars for this country, who suffered unemployment and came out of that, who fought for, and won, a Health Service and the Beveridge Insurance Plan. These things had to be fought for, too, they were not just handed out as a generous bonus. Now our generation of pensioners built up the wealth of this country in order to be able to do these things, and therefore we are entitled as a right to a sufficient pension to live a decent life in the community with dignity.

What kind of support have you had from other parts of the organised trade union movement in this campaign?

As I have already mentioned, our Camden Pensioners' Association is sponsored by the Trades Council, which sends a representative to our Committee. They have given us money from time to time, because the 5p from the members doesn't go very far and we have to get money from other places, too. We have also had money from the Co-op Political Committee. In our Association, we have organised deputations to the Social Services Minister, and have had a demonstration outside Buckingham Palace. Together with other pensioners' organisations from all over the country, and the T U C, we also organised a lobby in November 1972 at the House of Commons, with a big meeting in the Albert Hall and, of course, we received a good deal of publicity for that. As we in Camden have three large stations where people were going to arrive from various parts of the country, we decided that Camden would give them all a welcome. We got the National Union of Railwaymen's rooms, with an overflow at the Transport and General Workers' Union rooms in Gower Street, thinking that five or six hundred pensioners would come. Well, we had 1,800 by the end of the day! We got the Mayor to come along and speak, and we kept having to rush out to buy bread and cheese as we kept running out of supplies. We had O A P s standing at the stations with banners telling people where to go and several taxi-drivers gave free rides to the pensioners—this got us a lot of publicity, too. Arising out of the lobby, we made contact with people all over the country who, like us, were trying to organise pensioners' organisations with a militant outlook.

And so Camden again took the initiative, and in May 1973 we called a conference in the St Pancras Assembly Rooms and asked for delegates from the pensioners' organisations contacts we had made at the lobby: 250 delegates came. Some people also came as observers, rather than as delegates representing the National O A P s' Association that's been going for a long number of years but hasn't been connected with the working-class movement or the trade unions, and therefore is more 'establishment' than anything else. At this conference it was agreed to set up a British Pensioners' and Trade Union Committee, and we then called the first meeting. We didn't want it to take over all the other groups, as we wanted them to carry on autonomously, but we wanted a co-ordinating committee, so we elected a chairman and secretary. I think you have to do that in big organisations; it's difficult to run them informally like a small community group. Then the North-western Federation of Trade Unions, particularly in Manchester and Liverpool, took up our suggestion of a lobby on the eve of the Trades Union Congress. We'd already got the support of the Transport and General Workers' Union and the Engineers' Union, but we wanted all the other unions as well, and something more than just a token 'Yes, we support you.'

And so it was from that Association that the demonstration of 20,000 people was held in Blackpool. The T U C passed not only the resolution of support but also a resolution that it would consider industrial action to help us.

Arising from that, a small delegation went from the British Pensioners' Committee to the Labour Party Congress in October. And then the Labour Party committed itself to support the pensioners and even said that, maybe, by the time the Labour Party came to power again, the pension would need to be more than the £10 and £16 we were asking for. Of course, they didn't know then about the February 1974 election. So what we have done with this co-ordinating committee is to get the T U C committed, even to the point of industrial action, and the Labour Party fully committed. The next step was a conference here in London in December 1973 called by the Labour Party to discuss the next plans for action to advance the cause of the old age pensioners. This is what we have been doing on the political side. While we are non-party-political as an organisation, we are not non-political, because the only way the O A P s will get more money is through Parliament passing a Bill to that effect.

Has this political campaign involved you in any difficulties with some of your members because you might be seen to be too closely identified with one particular political party?

No—we haven't had the problem of some of us thinking we are becoming too much identified with the Labour Party. Most of our people just feel that they want this decent pension so much that they are prepared to let anybody or any party help them. I think they have only sorrow that the other parties haven't identified themselves as much as with their cause. In Scotland they have had an O A P s' organisation for several years which began to revive and become really active only when a member of the Communist Party, an ex-miners' leader and one or two others began to participate. Still, on the other hand, it's a great step forward that the trade unions have now definitely committed themselves, instead of just passing resolutions as they did in the past. Some of the unions, particularly the Transport and General Workers' Union, have also set up O A P committees of their members because the pensioners themselves have now become more active and have forced the unions to accept that they must help the pensioners. We have said to them that they will be O A P s themselves one day and have an interest in organising to rectify the present position before they get to that stage. On this point of links with the unions, it has been infinitely important that people like myself have been active trade unionists and known how to talk to trade unionists. In fact, most of the people active in the OAPS' organisation up and down the country have been ex-trade-union officials.

Wales has started a very active OAPS' association with another miners' leader who is also a Communist Party member. In the Coventry area the key organisers are ex-Transport and General Workers' Union members as in the Birmingham area, while in the Manchester area, they are ex-textile workers. And it has been this influx of experienced people who started their organisations from the grass roots, like we did in Camden, who have now built up our big pensioners' association which has induced, if not forced, the TUC and the Labour Party to come out in our favour. A terrific step forward for the pensioners.

What about link-ups between the pensioners and other organisations and agencies, particularly those based on community rather than workplace issues?

We haven't been very active with other organisations in the community—for instance, tenants' associations—maybe because old people have come to us rather than them thinking we understand their problems better. The Social Services departments have given us some help in providing a room to meet in, as they have done elsewhere in the borough, I understand, but that is all. They don't come to our meetings or discuss anything with us. We would like them to come if they didn't try to run the thing. I'm not saying they're not doing a good job, in the main, but our experience of these people is that they think they know best. Agencies in the community, which are there to help, often like to tell people what they think they ought to do. Well, the old people have been told for too long what to do and what not to do, and one of the basic characteristics of our organisation is that we don't tell them what they ought to do. We ask them what they want, and what their problems are, and we discuss these together. And it is because we discuss these together we are getting somewhere. Now, I'm not sure if I ought to say this, but although some of these other voluntary organisations have been very helpful, they also tend to try and tell the branches what they should do. The local Neighbourhood Centre certainly appears to have this attitude. As a result, in that area, since the council is building a new community centre, the Malden Road branch is going to meet there, rather than at the Neighbourhood Centre, so that they will be on their own, as we are, with nobody to tell them what to do. They are all very well-meaning, but they all have their own ideas. I don't think they realise this, but they can't resist organising. I heard a rumour that one Neighbourhood Centre said that the Camden O A P S were far too militant and that they weren't going to have anything to do with them.

We haven't had a lot to do with the Law Centre so far, although I think that some of our members have gone along there with their individual problems. Right at the beginning of the Law Centre, I invited the director to come and speak to us about what they hoped to be and do. The community worker from there has also been to talk to us. She is trying to get group cases, and so far we haven't had a group case as such, because, you see, if there's a housing group case, for instance, I think the tenants' association would take it up.

Do you have any words of caution for community workers, then, as to how best to be helpful to the pensioners?

I'll speak about the voluntary agencies first, although it applies to community professional workers, too. They are very kind, but old people don't want to be set apart, and this is one of the things in our Camden organisation that we've really stressed: old people need to be, and should be, an integral part of the community. The Social Services can help by providing home helps, district nurses and other assistance. But one of the biggest things for people confined to their houses is the loneliness: I think the professional workers should be discussing this particular problem, not just seeing that the district nurse goes to visit. This is what happens: she goes and maybe stops half an hour, the home help goes and stops maybe an hour; but the elderly are awake twelve hours in a day as a rule, and what do they do with the rest of their time when they can't get out of the house? There needs to be discussion on how this problem can be tackled. It's not easy; all they have is the television, and they get sick of it sometimes because it can't talk back to them. And I know some of the community people say: 'She talks my head off when I go.' Well, why? Because it's the only talk she's having. I think they should at all costs avoid segregating people, and try to persuade an old person who lives next door or up the street, who can go out, to get to know someone who can't. Old people want gossip. Community workers should help to put old people in touch with the local network rather than tell their organisations what to do. The trouble with a lot of the clubs run for old people is that they are run *for* them and not *by* them. And so, in a way, the clubs actually cut them off from the rest of the community. If someone comes along to try to make them active to fight for a better pension, it's not liked at all, because the clubs are run on the basis of keeping the pensioners passive and treating them like nitwits who don't understand the problems of the day; just entertaining them with outings and Christmas parties, etc. Whereas what we're trying to do in the Camden Pensioners' and the British pensioners' organisations is to involve the pensioners in the community so that they know what's going on—they have something to contribute, they have a wealth of experience and knowledge which could be invaluable, if only it were properly used.